THE BLUEBELLS
AND OTHER VERSE

THE WORKS OF JOHN MASEFIELD

PLAYS

The Faithful
Good Friday
Tristan and Isolt
Easter
Melloney Holtspur

A King's Daughter
The Trial of Jesus
The Tragedy of Nan
The Coming of Christ
End and Beginning

POETRY

Dauber
The Daffodil Fields
Philip the King
Lollingdon Downs
A Poem and Two Plays
Reynard the Fox
Enslaved
Right Royal
Selected Poems (new edition)
King Cole

Poems (collected)
Midsummer Night
Minnie Maylow's Story
A Tale of Troy
A Letter from Pontus
Gautama the Enlightened
Wonderings
Natalie Maisie and Pavilastukay
On the Hill
The Bluebells and Other Verse

FICTION

Sard Harker
Odtaa
The Midnight Folk
The Hawbucks
The Bird of Dawning
The Taking of the Gry
The Box of Delights

Victorious Troy
Eggs and Baker
The Square Peg
Dead Ned
Live and Kicking Ned
Basilissa
Conquer

GENERAL

Gallipoli
The Old Front Line
St. George and the Dragon
The Battle of the Somme
Recent Prose
With the Living Voice
The Wanderer of Liverpool
Poetry: A Lecture
So Long to Learn

The Conway
The Nine Days Wonder
In the Mill
New Chum
Thanks Before Going and A
    Macbeth Production
A Book of Both Sorts
A Book of Prose Selections
William Shakespeare

JOHN MASEFIELD

★

THE BLUEBELLS

AND OTHER VERSE

HEINEMANN

LONDON MELBOURNE TORONTO

William Heinemann Ltd

LONDON   MELBOURNE   TORONTO

CAPE TOWN   AUCKLAND

THE HAGUE

First published 1961

© by John Masefield 1961

Printed in Great Britain
by The Windmill Press Ltd
Kingswood, Surrey

CONTENTS

1.	The Bluebells	1
2.	The Starry Night	4
	The Night of Kings	7
	The Song of Gaspar	36
3.	Ossian	37
4.	Eighty-Five to Win	73
5.	Odysseus Tells	82
6.	King Edward the Second Tells his Story	106
7.	A Cry to Music	121
8.	The Princess Malinal	122
9.	Memories	132
10.	Middle Farm, or The Cherries	135
11.	In Praise of Nurses	140
12.	The Hawthorns at the Chantry Door	143
13.	Question and Answer	152
14.	King Edward the Confessor and his Ring	162
15.	The Buried Bride	166
16.	John Grimaldi	170
17.	A Word with Sir Francis Drake	178
18.	On the Shipwreck of Sir Cloudesley Shovell	186
19.	On H.M.S. *Calliope* at Apia	191
20.	On Pilots	195
21.	Captain Barnaby	200

THE BLUEBELLS

We stood upon the grass beside the road,
At a wood's fence, to look among the trees.
In windless noon the burning May-time glowed.
Gray, in young green, the beeches stood at ease.
Light speckled in the wood or left it dim:
There lay a blue in which no ship could swim,
Within whose peace no water ever flowed.

Within that pool no shadow ever showed;
Tideless was all that mystery of blue.
Out of eternities man never knew
A living growth man never reaped nor sowed
Snatched in the dim its fitness from the hour
A miracle unspeakable of flower
That tears in the heart's anguish answered-to.

How paint it; how describe? None has the power.
It only had the power upon the soul
To consecrate the spirit and the hour,
To light to sudden rapture and console,
Its beauty called a truce: forgave: forgot
All the long horror of man's earthly lot,
A miracle unspeakable of flower
In a green May unutterably blue.

I

For what, for whom, was all the beauty spread,
This colour, that had power to dissolve
Man's fugitive dismays into resolve
And be a balsam upon hearts that bled?
In all the mile of marvel, what immense
Current of life had power so intense
To wrest such bounty out of sun and soil?
What starved imagination ached to feed?
What harassed heart implored for an assoil?

Who can behold it on this lonely hill,
Here in the one week when the wonder shows,
Here, where old silence waits on the wind's will,
Where, on the track, none but the postman goes,
Where upon mouse or bird the kestrel drops,
Or spotted 'pecker burrowing his bill
Furrows the bark, or the red squirrel hops
Or hunting vixen lifts a questing nose,
What other seer can the beauty thrill?

None, in the day; and, when the beauty dims,
When moonlight makes the still un-leafy tree,
A spell-bound ghost that cannot move his limbs,
What other passer can be here to see?
The new-come night-jar chirring on the branch?
The nightingale exulting in his hymns?
The wood-mice flitting where the moon-beams blanch?
The wind, in the few fir-trees, like a sea
On which the pale owl like a feather swims?

For none of these can such a marvel be.

Has it a source in a forgotten scene?
Is it a mark of vital methods taken,
Of choices made, at turning-points of Fate
Whether to know the Earth or seek the Queen?
Is it but yearly gladness of bonds shaken?
After a prison, an apparent gate?
Or is this miracle of blue and green
A symbolling of what it all may mean,
When the Queen comes and all we dead awaken?

THE STARRY NIGHT

That starry Night when Christ was born,
The shepherds watched by Dead Man's Thorn;
They shared their supper with the dogs,
And watched the sparks flick from the logs
Where the coppings from the holly burned.

Then the dogs growled, and faces turned
To horsemen, coming from the hill.

A Captain called to them, 'Keep still . . .
We're riding, seeking for a sign
That human beings are divine . . .
Is there such marvel, hereabout?'

The shepherds said, 'Us don't know nowt.
We're Mr Jones's shepherd chaps.
Old Mr Jones might know, perhaps . . .
But if you've come this country road,
You've passed his house and never knowed.
There's someone in the town might know;
A mile on, keeping as you go.'

Long after all had disappeared,
More horsemen (from the woodland), neared;
And one, a King, with a dark skin,
Cried, 'Friends, are gods and men akin?

A wonder tells of this, they say.
Is it near here? Is this the way?'

'Why, no' the shepherds said . . . 'Perhaps.
We're Mr Jones's shepherd chaps.
Old Mr Jones would know, I wis,
But he'll be gone to bed by this.'

After the troop had passed away,
A third came (from the River way)
And cried, 'Good friends, we seek to find
Some guidance for the questing mind,
Eternity, in all this Death,
Some life out-living flesh and breath.
Can we find this, the way we ride?'

'You'd better picket down and bide,'
The shepherds said 'And rest your bones.
We're shepherds here to Mr Jones.
When morning comes, you ask of he,
For he'd know more of that than we.
We're only shepherds here; so bide.'

'We cannot wait,' the horseman cried.
'Life cannot wait; Death cannot stay;
This midnight is our only day.
Push on, friends; shepherds all, farewell.
This living without Life is Hell.'

The clatter of the horse-hoofs failed,
Along the wood a barn-owl wailed;
The small mice rustled in the wood;
The stars burned in their multitude.

Meanwhile, within the little town,
The camping horsemen settled down;
The horses drank at stream and fed
On chaff, from nose-bags, picketed.
The men rolled blankets out, and stretched;
Black Nim their hard cheese supper fetched;
Then, after spirit from the gourd,
Each turned to sleep without a word,
But shortly roused again to curse
A some-one calling for a nurse
To help a woman in her woe.

All this was very long ago.

THE NIGHT OF KINGS

Melchior

    The shepherds, up on Dead Man's Wold,
    Heaped up the blaze against the cold;
    They told their dogs to watch the sheep
    And settled under rugs to sleep
    But wondered what the star could mean
    Where no such star had ever been.
    'It must mean summat,' as they said,
    'Somebody being born, or dead,
    Or else a war, or else a pest . . . ,
    "Leave dogs and stars alone is best,"
    My granfer said, and he said true.
    That King and them there other two,
    Were star-struck, mad as the March hare.'

    A mile thence, in the market-square
    The three troops, in the little town,
    In turn bought leave to settle down,
    Where space was, up and down a brook.

    The horses blew their oats and shook
    The tether-chains; the lanterns cast
    Odd gleams as men with buckets passed.
    The inn-doors slammed and jargon sped
    As strangers asked for beer and bread
    In strange speech, tending foreign pence

Of silver minted long leagues thence,
Stamped with a fish or barley ears.

'Friends, it is very many years,
Since I, King Melchior, pitched tent
In that star-riding that we went.
I was the first to come, and took
First pick of place and things to cook,
And having bribed and picked and bought,
"Now . . . supper and to bed," I thought.

But in the street there was a welter
Of later horsemen seeking shelter;
All men and horses, carts and jangle
In tumult hard to disentangle,
At midnight with so little light,
With town dogs looking for a bite,
The horses kicking at the press,
All stomachs crying Emptiness,
And all men swearing as they knocked
At house-doors nobody unlocked . . .

Most wisely . . . such a tumult made,
Mothers with daughters much afraid.

So, as the outfits milled and jammed,
And door-bolts clocked and windows slammed,
The Town-Reeve shouted through his hands:
'Where are the Captains? Who commands?

Sir? You? And you, Sir? Right . . . It's late . . .
You'd better picket down and bait
Here, in the market, where you are.
These cattle-pens will all unbar.
You, Sir, take that side. You, Sir, here.
And keep this centre gangway clear
To all the water; and set sentry
Both here and at the tavern entry.
And, please, no fires here, nor noise.
Your merry men must be good boys,
It's time that people settled down.
We're early risers here in town.'

Well, order followed when men heard
One definite commanding word . . .
I turned towards my camp for food
And passed by where two captains stood,
Outside a lighted door whose keepers
Swore that they could not shelter sleepers . . .
I liked their looks, so said 'Good friends . . .
My camp is just where the town ends . . .
There . . . at the light . . . do come with me . . .
I've food and blanketings for three . . .
Come dine with me, and drink a cup.
And rest abed till sun is up.'

This they were glad to do; we went
The less than furlong to the tent.

Within the busy grass the greed
Of horses, picketed at feed

Gave to the night a crunching sound
Of new snow trodden upon ground,
'My friends,' I said, 'Here we are met . . .
Three taken in a midnight net.
May we discover who we are?
No doubt, all following the star.
My name is Melchior, a King;

Baltasar
  'I'm Baltasar, the Wondering.'

Gaspar
  'I am Gaspar of the Broken Heart.'

Melchior
  'We come from many miles apart,'
I said, 'And all we wander by
Is just that portent in the sky.'

And truly, as we chattered thus
That portent seemed to blaze at us.
Its eye of flame was sinking down
To westward of the sleeping town.
It seemed to crackle as it went.
I said 'It's force will soon be spent.
It can be nought but flaming gas,
Burning a distant world, alas,
Not this, ah, no such luck, nor sense.
Just destiny and impotence.

But never heed it, friends; its light
Is only wonderful at night;

It is a nothingness by day,
The morning clears it all away.
There, down among the woods it wests.
Come in, to midnight supper, guests.

There, in the lighted tent, we fed,
But when I sent the hands to bed,
I brought out raisins, nuts and wine.

I said 'O comrades, guests of mine,
Here we are met, three wandering men
Unlikely to be here agen,
Unlikelier still to meet and share
An hour together anywhere,
Shall we, for this one hour, speak
Frankly, of what we know or seek,
Or shall we drink a cup instead
A night-cap cup, and so to bed?'

Both asked to linger and discuss
All sorts of questions troubling us.
They had not talked for days (nor I)
So there we talked the darkness by.
While Heaven wheeled its starry Wain.

I said: 'Now, I must ask again;
Not, who we are, but why we come
Riding a-questing far from home?'
And at that instant, footsteps neared
With people muttering a word,
So, looking out, I hailed a pair
In a hurry, with a lantern, there.

'What is it? Are you seeking me?'
'No, Captain,' said a man, 'Let be . . .
Doctor and Nurse, a child-birth case,
I' the byre, by the watering-place;
Some wandering woman in distress.'

'I hope your services may bless
And all go well: good night,' said I.

'Good night,' they said, and hurried by.

Beyond their stilling steps, I heard
The water murmuring her word.
I said 'I wished them well, indeed.
And yet I loathe this mortal seed;
Ever new birth, never new sense,
But something here and going hence
As silly as the brook that goes
From underworlds that no man knows
To seas unseen and leaves no trace
Save other water in its place . . .

Now, here, another senseless mite
Flung headlong to this losing fight.
Dragged by a thoughtless instant's lust
To struggle life-long for a crust,
And curse his getters; sure the worst
Curst, are the getters of the curst.

But we, who oft have cursed our sires,
Are here, bedevilled by desires.

Well . . . what desires drive us so?
What are we seeking? May we know?'

Then Baltasar: 'Sir, you should lead.'

I said: 'A remedy for need . . .
I seek for God, that is, a light
In life's abominable night.
No light comes from the present party
Of Mithras, Baal and Astarte.
Marduk, Shumalia, the Sphinx . . .
The sparrow hatches in their chinks.
Egyptian Nilus, Hathor, Ptah,
And all that were and all that are,
Are man-made figments, climate-tinged,
Appealed-to, when the time's unhinged,
By daftness, with as much effect
As flies have, when the Bird has pecked.

Men need the gods, and made the lot,
The snaky, birdy, thin and squat,
The bull-y, crocodile-y, blast-y,
The lame, the drunken and the nasty,
The toothy, bite-y, smite-y, gory,
Also the lustful and the whorey.

I ask you, what of light we find
In such abortions of the mind?

My own land's gods survive, being Greek,
And yet I am ashamed to speak

13

Of things that men believe they did.
I seek a god at present hid.

One, such a King above all Kings,
As shall inspire splendid things,
A ruler putting down all crime,
A bringer of a golden time,
A spirit splendid with such state
That every man will imitate
With perfectness in all things done.
A soul in people like the sun.
A glory for whom men will die,
A Light that puts all darkness by.

That star there, that we stopped to see,
These idiots say that this is He,
Himself, in triumph, coming soon,
Riding in fire on a moon . . .

Myself, I think some burning gas
Makes Heaven brighter than it was
But still, in this last month, the word
Has spread, however much absurd,
That it is He, and that the wise
Must follow where His banner flies.
So here I am, and here are we,
Soon we shall come upon the sea
And have to turn: perhaps by then
The gas will be burnt out agen.

It is not wholly folly, this.
In every crowd some wisdom is.

On every road by which we pass
Are some who seek this burning gas.
My hope is, that among them, one
Will know a god who's like a Sun,
A god transfiguring, creating,
Impelling and illuminating;
One like all beauty, life and power,
At once a stem and fruit and flower,
One that will make men men indeed,
And clear man's sorry soil of weed.

If such a god be known and named,
His truths shall surely be proclaimed.
I will proclaim them, though they bring
Upheaval both to realm and King.
No matter: such a god will mend
Man's filthy errors in the end.

Such is my seeking: what is yours?

Baltasar
This world of ailments needing cures
Seeks deities whose ministries
May bring an ending to disease.
Perhaps, if this new star be sign
Of change that deathless wills design,
Some such divineness may be brought
As living faith in human thought.
That would change much.
                    The god you seek
Would crack the systems grown antique,

15

But might he not be too much male?
If strength and force turn many a scale,
Women and children, too, demand
A guiding friend and helping hand.
Perhaps your manly god might seem
Too like the pious Spartan's dream,
Sublime for spearmen, dogs and brothers,
But not for girls and nursing mothers.

But, there, I come, like you, to find
Some vision of a seeing mind,
Who shows a way that men may tread
Not broken-hearted by the dead,
Not blind to what to do, not mean,
Not snarling, hating and unclean . . .
Not dangerous with sex and sect,
Nor all astray with intellect.
I hope to find a lighted way
And lead men to it, if I may.

Melchior
And you, Sir; may we learn from you?

Gaspar
I seek for hope to make anew
My purpose, that a death has killed.

Most human lives are unfulfilled,
All human lives have something fine,

16

Some touch of what we call divine,
The men, a power, strength or art,
Women, a nobleness of heart.
This godlike quality survives
(Surely it must) our dying lives.
Is it not God, or all that is
God, in this sea of miseries?
In praying God, do we not pray
To souls beloved gone away,
Who tried, with unsuccess, at things
Vital to men (the art of Kings),
Who bore, with courage and with beauty,
The hatefulness of pain and duty?
Do not men think this star that burns
Is rested spirit that returns,
To cleanse and vivify and change
This life that silly creeds derange?'

Into the tent, there sprang a stranger
The Doctor who had passed us by.

The Doctor
    Captains, that woman is in danger.
    Heart failure, cold, and like to die . . .
    Can you spare wine and blankets?

Melchior
                      Take . . .

The Doctor
    My thanks, for the poor creature's sake.

17

Melchior
  Can we do more?

The Doctor
                Yes: if things mend.
  Pray that good spirits may attend.

Melchior
  Call to us, if you need: we'll hear.

The Doctor
  Thank God, you happened to be near.

Baltasar
  Alack, what avenues of fear
  Our mothers tread alone, to bring
  Man's destiny to sot and King.

Gaspar
  What agonies of life they take
  For thoughtless men's unworthy sake.

Melchior
  Yes; and what agonies they make.

  They bring the children without whom
  This earth would be the last man's tomb.
  A manless stretch of Paradise,
  The grass, and happy dogs, and flies.
  But women propagate and breed
  This squalor, mixed of lies and greed,

This infamy of Man, whose lot,
Condemns whoever was begot
To grieve, blaspheme and sin, till death
Annuls his pestilence of breath.
However much men mar or mend,
Death brings them to an utter end,
An end to doing good and sinning.
Whose primal error was beginning.

Gaspar
I cannot think the lovely die.

Melchior
Ah, friend, the sweetness of a lie,
May soothe a broken heart, indeed,
But the dead cease, and the hearts bleed.
Even my own has sorely bled
Seeking the dear beloved dead;
But no least comfort came, or comes.
The dead have had their martyrdoms,
Leave them at peace.
                 I knew one case
And only one, in any place,
Of one dead creature who contrived
A way of shewing he survived.
The thing they call a ghost, or sprite,
Who roams the owl-time and at night.
There was a mongrel robber-chief,
Bandit, and horse-and-cattle thief,
Ruffian at any sort of crime
I' the west there, in my younger time.

I sent out men who broke the gang.
This robber-chief they did not hang
But cut his head off, there and then.

That fellow's spirit haunted men.
Just by the grave at which he died,
He would jump up at even-tide,
His cut head tucked beneath his arm.
It caused the passers much alarm,
This hopper with a headless neck,
This cock who could no longer peck,
But still could terrify, and worse.
His ghost became a public curse;
Men would not use the road at night,
For many folk had seen the sight
Or swore they had, or thought they had.
I promised them I'd lay the lad.

Mind: I supposed that tricks were played
By urchins making folk afraid.
The half-seen, in uncertain light,
Is all the ghost in human fright
And boys, I judged, caused this half-seen.
Well . . . off I travelled to the scene,
A barren trackway on the wold,
With twisted thorn-trees bleak with cold.
No ambush there for boys at all,
A grave beside a ruined wall,
And just the wind and loneliness,
Where justice had killed wickedness.

I stood at sentry-go all night
Three nights together on the site,
Full-moony nights, but no ghost hopped.

I said 'His frolics shall be stopped
This spiritual frog shall end.'

I dug him up, that buried friend,
There lay he, skull within his arm.
I said 'You'll do no further harm.'
I had him down the hill perforce,
Let build a mighty heap of gorse
And burned him into ash, and shook
The ashes in a running brook.

I had his grave filled-in and fire
Burned on it in another pyre.

Then I proclaimed: 'After today,
Man, woman, child, who dares to say
That she, he, it, saw this thing hop,
Shall shackle to a post and stop
One week on what was once his grave.

I heard no more about the Knave.

That's the one instance known to me
Of corpse who somehow seemed to be
Alive in some way, although dead,
I quenched his shadow-life by dread.

To me, the Dead are gone; but you . . .
So young, so gallant, haply knew
Some unbelievable sweet scrap
Of soul surviving mortal hap?
Has such a blessing come to you?

Gaspar
Ah, never, never any sign
Able to calm this grief of mine.
But was there not that King of Spain
Whose dear dead Queen came back again?
In her, he had lost everything,
For who is lonely as a King?
His agony of grief so sped
It called his love back from the dead.
She came again, white, sad and dim;
Men saw her bless and talk to him.
More than a year she lingered so,
Saying what none will ever know,
Keeping him sane, keeping him willed,
To govern, though his heart was killed.
Then, presently, she was not there,
There was no shadow in the air,
That mist of woman was no more.

Death is a grim dividing door
That shuts and keeps its tenants fast.

He knew her presence could not last,
And trembled (as they say) for dread
Lest he were prisoning the dead,
Keeping her here on earth un-free.

No spirit has appeared to me.

Baltasar
　A dead friend came to me in dream.
　It was his very self, I deem
　No phantom, but his living light.
　He shone upon me in the night.

　Zeus has decreed that I must guide
　Some thousands in a country-side,
　Rough mountaineers and sea-port men,
　Tillers and farmers of the glen,
　A rude lot, poorly kinged, Zeus knows.

　Two years past, pestilence arose,
　And like a mountain-fire spread.
　Whole villages were stricken dead
　And no drug served, and no man knew
　What caused this running thing that slew,
　For it was swift death, riding post
　As secret as a daylight ghost,
　And fataller than war, or flood.
　The poison got into the blood
　How, no man knew; and then you died.

　I being but their servant, tried
　All things that might perhaps avail,
　But death on death I saw them fail;
　No drug seemed even to delay
　The power of the thing to slay.
　So there I rode the land, and said

23

'O Zeus, put me among the dead,
For since I cannot guard my trust,
I am but dust, unroyal dust,
Unlit by a divine bright gleam.'

Then in the night there came a dream
My friend appeared, in light, and said:
'By tainted water this is spread.
The upper springs are pure: drink those.'

He seemed within a golden rose
Made out of life; he smiled; he drew
Back to the rose's deepest hue,
And there was I alone, but knowing
Salvation from his spirit's showing.

I called out guards: I sent out word:
Ere the cocks crowed or pigeons stirred,
All water-points were sentinelled.
From that bright dream the curse was quelled.

Vagrants had fouled the duct that brings
Our waters from the central springs.
The upper springs were not involved.
My peoples' problem was resolved.
That my friend helped me, I am certain.
What we call Death is but a curtain.

Melchior
    Yet, out of all Earth's millions gone
    What stands for men to build upon?

We three all long for God: and yet
What living presence have we met
To show that such exist and are?
Not yonder very splendid star,
But known, and here?
                      I maintain, none.
I know I never met with one
Save Destiny, that gave me rule
Over my land of freak and fool
A duty that I try to do;
Has any god appeared to you?

Baltasar
    No. I have sought, but never found.
I visit consecrated ground
In shrines and temples, and have heard
An oracle's ambiguous word;
And heard a pythoness declare
That spirits were in presence there,
And that the spirits present said
That they were spirits of men dead.
And some of these have seemed to me
Deceivers of credulity.

But faith remains that in the end
The curtain of our night will rend,
And light illumine what is dark.
Light IS, for we perceive a spark . . .
And are the better men thereby,
Myself am better, even I . . .
I have learned patience; perhaps more.

I have met nothing to adore
Seen neither Light nor Shape, and heard
No Wisdom's overwhelming Word
Nor quaked with any special grace
In any consecrated place.
But yet at times, in hills, at springs,
A hint of everlasting things
Is present, somehow, in the scene,
As though immortal King or Queen
Were there, remote, but yet akin
And shedding fuller life therein.
Many have felt this, far from men,
Beside the water in a glen
Where none but deer or curlews drink.
Or at a precipice's brink
Where the hawk mews and the wind whistles
And sheep skulls glare in the grass bristles.

I know not what to call the sign
Save evidence of the divine.
Many such spots still have a shrine
And some, great temples, sought by many.

But you, Sir, named one godlike thing,
The Destiny that made you King.
You feel that some Divine Hand sets
All palms and crowns and coronets.
I think it; and that such Hand gave
The iron fettering the slave,
The sex all have to learn to bear . . .
And the time when, and the place where.

I think it . . . and admitting this . . .
Destiny governs all that is . . .
But what it is that governs so
I do not know, but long to know . . .
I think . . . our younger friend, should see
More clearly into Life than we . . .
What Divine Voice has he heard speak?

Gaspar
In truth, it is not God I seek
But Her who once was linked to me
By heart-annulling Destiny.
That Destiny most surely spoke
The day my love for her awoke.
It will seem childish, spoken here. . .
Within my heart a voice spoke clear
Bidding me buy a colt for sale.

No man so sternly told could fail
To follow the command: I bought . . .
The Fortune of my Life was wrought
In that one purchase, Love, Fame, Power.
All from five seconds in an hour
Not otherwise a startling thing.

It brought me love, made me a King,
Crowned me in all ways with success.
The horse was Fortune's self no less . . .
I rode him in the Sacred Race,
Along the Old Gods' trysting-place,
Through Seven Fires and won, and won.

But this would weary everyone.
I say 'A Spirit spoke to me
Knowing that certain things would be
The greater things of Destiny,
Therefore a God'.

      No other sign
Of God has moved this heart of mine.
Their lives must be remote from ours
Where autumn never dims the flowers
And sin is not, and Death is not.
Why should they heed our mortal lot?

What can we be to spirits pure
Who know the future and endure?
Nothing I fear: it is too plain.
Yet He that spoke may speak again.'

Melchior

So, Sir, you won the Sacred Race . . .?
I watched that once, by Zeus's grace,
There on the downs where skylarks sing
And burning gorse-flakes fly and sting.
An old religious rite still done
Riding through fire . . . and you won?
Won, on a god-appointed horse.

We touch some transitory force,
As it appears: your friend who told
How running Death could be controlled:
Your god there at the sale who knew
What that one colt might be to you.

And my old thief whom I made stop
Living and when he used to hop.
You have been luckier than I:
I have no answer to the why,
No, not to any of the whys
That mortal sorrows emphasize
Or mortal madnesses inflame.
To me, Life cannot be a game
Played by a god or by the dead;
It is a kennel of beasts fed
By rapine of their fellow-beasts;
It is a pan of working yeasts
That never will be bread or food . . .
And any pestilence that strewed
The lot as corpses everywhere,
I say, would make the world more fair.
Let's see the Night, now men are still.'

The water lapsed over the sill,
And in some roost or pigeon-loft
A bird gurgled and fluttered soft;
The night was drawing to a close.
And overhead a murmur rose
Of migrant birds upon the wing
Returning north with twittering.
Steps sounded on the cobbled lane.

'I am the Doctor come again,'
A voice said: 'You have saved two lives.
Observe the strangeness life contrives

Blind darkness, and a girl in need
Of vital stimulant at speed
And unexpected you at hand.
And but for you the running sand
Would have run out: they would be dead.

Your things are in the cattle-shed,
The Nurse will see that they're returned.

Well, truly, one thing I have learned
The Unexpected Way is Fate's.'

Melchior
My friend, the strangers at the gates
Are often Gods, so proverbs say.
Sit, Sir, and drink.'

The Doctor
                    'I cannot stay,
Two minutes; but I'll sit and drink.
You haven't been abed, I think
And now: it's nearly morning: lo,
The valley cocks begin to crow.'

And surely from the distance dim
The valley-farm cocks answered him,
Faint challenges, and hopes that said
'The morning's coming: who's afraid?
We'll be let out: we can go scrout
The dew-drops from the clover-sprout.
And peck the little things we scare.'

30

Then Baltasar: 'The woman there . . .
Has she no home? Has she no friends?'

The Doctor
  'Nothing but what her Fortune sends.
  That (having sent you) must be good.
  If you could spare a little food
  It might be kind.

Baltasar   Some shall be sent.

Melchior
  Doctor, before you reached the tent
  We talked of gods and deaths and lives
  And whether anything survives
  The worn-out perished mortal man.

The Doctor
  I hope: but know not how it can.
  Though men are animals, their minds
  Have powers not of beastly kinds
  There is some essence that is strange.
  Possibly that survives the change.
  My task concerns what lives and dies.

Melchior
  The maggots and more loathsome flies.

The Doctor
  Not that, where governments are wise,
  Some prudent states have given heed
  To who shall be allowed to breed.

As yet, they never breed for sense,
Only for troops for their defence.

Baltasar
　Perhaps good animals at least.

The Doctor
　A sort of strong blind stupid beast
　Who credits what the statesmen say,
　And can endure and will obey.

Melchior
　A better type perhaps than that
　You saved, the homeless woman's brat.

The Doctor
　Why, even as to that, who knows?
　What governs dice-cubes in the throws?
　Not what the will wills or mind meant
　But Fate, or Chance her instrument.
　That this child's Fate is good is clear
　From being born when you were near:
　Without that, who can say indeed?

　But here's the morning: I must speed,
　There is a man in pain, out west,
　I must attempt to give him rest
　Before my morning cases call.

　Farewell, and thank you one and all.

32

It would be kind if you could spare
Some something to the woman there.
The Nurse is there: the best Nurse known.'

Melchior resumes
　　At this, he left us three alone,
　　And passed over the grass away.
　　'Ah, friends,' I said, 'It's nearly day.
　　What would you care for? Bed and rest?'
　　They said, to join their men were best,
　　But thanked me, and prepared to go.

　　I said 'Wait still, until we know
　　About this woman and have left
　　Some havings, since she seems bereft.
　　The gold-dust, spice and gums we bring,
　　In these wild parts buy anything
　　Let us bring some of those to her.'

　　So, with some gum and gold and myrrh,
　　Some woollens, honey, eggs and cake,
　　And that dried meat the westerns make,
　　We started for the cattle-byre.
　　The Nurse had lit a little fire,
　　She saw us coming, checked, and cried . . .

The Nurse
　　'Let the two sleep, O Kings, abide.
　　But carol, for the spirit tells
　　That in eternity the bells
　　Are ringing for this morning's sake.

Another King has come to take
Life's bitter death to help mankind.'

Melchior
Nurse, we are three astray and blind,
Seeking a thing we hope to find
But have not yet found: never may . . .
Now that poor woman in the hay,
All harrowed into death's door thus,
Is somehow linked to all of us.
We would leave gifts for when she wakes
For the child's and for her suffering's sakes.
May she hope on: I leave this gold.

Baltasar
May good hope keep both child and her . . .
I leave them this all-buying myrrh.

Gaspar
May she hope on . . . I give alone
What one had given had she known.

Melchior
Then, as we turned, my batman brought
A heap of things, and said 'We thought . . .
. . . The fellows thought, my lord, that these
Might bless them with a little ease.

The Nurse
She'll thank you all; more than you know.

Melchior
> We bowed and as we turned to go
> A breathing of the morning took
> The mist above the little brook,
> And shook the dew drops from the branch.
> The eastward sky began to blanch,
> The budded beech became distinct
> Like script on parchment sharply inkt.
> The peacocks in their splendour flew
> Into the grass flashing the dew,
> And then a bell began, and then
> The footsteps of the bakers' men,
> The jangle of the milking-pails.
> And we, who had to ride, rode on,
> From Ilion to Avalon,
> To cities promised from towns gone.

THE SONG OF GASPAR

THE YOUNGEST OF THE THREE KINGS

I saw two towers in the light
Heaped with the apples of delight
All burning gold;

And SHE, of excellence untold
In robes unutterably bright
Stepped live, stepped bold.

O Excellence, unthanked, unsung,
Come from Eternity to tongue
What cannot die,
Love indestructible, youth-young,
Earth-deep, Heaven-high.

OSSIAN

PART I

Finn's Wooing
Grania

All this began because Finn wished to wed.
He was lonely, old and covetous of power,
He dreamed of empire with himself as head,
With eastern Eire pledged to him as dower.
Birth, Beauty, Wit ... which girl
Of all the land's princesses was the flower?
'Grania,' men said, 'the High-King Cormac's Daughter.'
Such was the human prelude to the slaughter.

So, calling Ossian, his wondrous Son,
And Dermot, noblest of his men at arms,
He said 'Go see if Cormac may be won
To grant this Princess of so many charms
To me, to be my Wife.
Dower of money down and dairy farms,
That may be settled later as is due,
I shall not care if he refuses you,

But should care, if I went myself to ask
And were refused; so go, and put the case.'
Ossian and Dermot went upon their task

To High-King Cormac in his dwelling-place
On Tara's watch-tower-hill.
And near the hill a Lady of great grace
Rode to them, saying, 'Ossian, son of Finn,
May Fortune bless your plea, lest ills begin.'

She was a Princess, beautiful and young,
With wreaths of gold-leaf wound about her hair,
Her gladness cannot well be told by tongue
Nor in her heart what depths of goodness were.
No wisdom such as hers
Comes often here as mortals were aware,
She rode an earth-disdaining horse whose pride
Showed in each step that such a Queen should ride.

Then Ossian, thanking her, replied 'Princess,
If you are Grania, as I surely deem,
May every happy Fortune deeply bless
My Father's proffer for your heart's esteem,
And as my Father's Son,
I say your beauty is beyond all dream,
And we, O Grania, will obey your rule
You being crowned as Queen to Finn MacCoul.'

'Ossian,' she said, 'Grania is on the Hill,
Ride forward to King Cormac with your suit,
May ever-changing Fortune have the will
To bring this plea of Finn's to happy fruit.
At present, Fortune sways,
The oracles are dumb, the seers mute,
Myself am Niamh of the Glittering Plain.
Our ways are one, and we shall meet again.

Then west away she rode, and Dermot said . . .
'Well, we have seen a wonder, you and I.
I thought her Grania, too, that lovely maid,
A body and soul to measure beauty by.'
Then, entering the Court,
They pled their cause, and Cormac made reply.
'It is for Grania's self to choose her mate.
Finn shall be welcome here to try his fate.'

With banners and with gifts Finn took his guard
And Tara-wards he rode to see and woo.
Ossian was with him, Dermot, Fand, the bard,
Osgar, the loveliest lad earth ever knew,
Bald Conan, the sharp-tongued,
Great-hearted Goll, whom later the sands slew,
Swift-footed Caoilte, too, yet all attest
That Dermot, nicknamed Love-Spot, was the best.

To Cormac's palace all were welcomed-in.
Grania, the love-bird, from her golden cage,
Earth's loveliest woman stepped to talk to Finn,
An old gray warrior more than thrice her age,
Who sought her as a prop
In cunning schemes he plotted to engage.
All this she pondered as the harps were loud,
And Finn embraced her, watched by all the crowd.

And at the feast that followed, though her smile
Was all for Finn, her thoughts were otherwhere,
Westward from Tara many a stony mile
With other love than veteran with white hair
Grown old in blood and drink.

39

Behind her smile an evil did prepare.
Niamh among the guests, who watched her well,
Half judged her purpose, so the stories tell.

When loving-cups had passed and singings ceased,
And dying torches marked the evening's end,
And all the royalties had left the feast,
Niamh drew near to Ossian, saying 'Friend,
Forgive, if I beseech . . .
Most perilously, evil things impend.
You, as Finn's son, may stop their making head.'
'Lady, I'll try . . . what is it that you dread?'

'Would that Fate told,' she cried, 'But, O, contrive . . .
That Dermot be away from here tonight.
Nothing but this will keep him man alive.
Send him with message out of speech and sight.'
'Conan commands the guard,
I, as Finn's son, have neither weight nor right . . .
To order anyone to go or stay . . .'
Ossian replied, 'Ask Conan . . . Conan may.'

But here the Warden of the High-King's State
Cried the command: 'Fianna, mount the guard
Till dawn tomorrow beside Tara Gate.'
All hurried thence, the heavy gates were barred,
The rampart lanterns lit.
The quiet of the midnight many-starred
Set all asleep save Conan's little band,
Dermot, the Ossians, Caoilte, Goll and Fand.

These in the guard-house just within the wall,
Arranging two to wake and five to rest,
The seven settled ready for a call,
To sleep or play the chess-game as seemed best.
A lantern lit the room.
The moon and stars went down into the west.
Upon the rampart-top the leisured feet
Of sentries crunched the gravel on their beat.

And then, as Ossian wondered by the gate
What horror, of all horrors, could impend
On Dermot, least deserving of ill fate,
A woman's voice cried 'May a very friend
Bid the night-watch good night?'
And Grania entered, putting sudden end
To wonder and to talk, for no man there
Had stood so near to any face more fair,

As exquisitely graceful as a snake
She glid into the room as all arose.
Beauty like hers made many hearts to ache
Her beauty quickened all the hearts of those,
She greeted Conan first,
Then, by the instinct that a beauty knows
She greeted each man there, or asked the name . . .
And each man thrilled, but wondered why she came.

And Ossian, thinking about Niamh's fear
For Dermot's safety, wondered all the more . . .
'My Father's bride-to-be, yet coming here . . .
At midnight to the watchers at the door . . .

O exquisite fair face,
Lovely as ever mortal woman bore . . .
Are you not come ill-omened as the moon,
That shines and brings the tides but dwindles soon?'

Each of the seven guards was shrewdly eyed,
And very clearly read; she then said this:
'You, the Fianna, are the Kingdom's pride . . .
Your Knightly Order, tell me what it is . . .?
What binds you each to each?'
Conan replied: 'Whatever is amiss
For King, or High-King, we are pledged to try
To combat, or reclaim, until we die.

That is our warrior-pledge, or part at least . . .
But many pledges are involved as well . . .
To share with all men present when we feast . . .
And Finn's trust never to betray nor tell . . .
Then at all times to aid
The suppliant asking, though it lead to hell,
And ever to help women in distress.
These are main duties: there are others less.'

She looked at them in turn: they all agreed.
Ossian and Goll suggested lesser things.
Then Grania said: 'O Dermot, take good heed . . .
I charge you by your Knightly promisings,
Take me at once away,
Out of this loathsome prison of the Kings
Westward, to where my Mother's people dwell . . .'
Upon the gate-guard instant horror fell.

Dermot stood stunned and trembling: very white.
'Lady' he said, 'that would be treachery . . .
Also desertion of my post tonight . . .
To take Finn's promised wife . . . I'd rather die . . .
It would be thing so base
All Eire's stablished state would fall awry . . .'
'I ask for Knightly service at your hands . . .'
'Princess, I am Finn's henchman, Finn commands . . .'

'But, no . . . I ask of you,' she answered him.
'A woman in distress seeks Knightly aid.
In dire distress, too; not from any whim.
You, not your Captain, took the oath you made.'
Here Conan interfered . . .
'The High King's orders have to be obeyed . . .
The gates are shut and nobody goes through,
Till dawn, that is the word: not even you.'

'There is no need to open any gate,'
Grania replied, 'there is a postern door . . .
Open all night for heralds going late . . .
I ask fulfilment of the oath you swore.'
'I am no herald, Queen,'
Dermot replied, 'But, as I said before,
To leave this guard-post ere the night is through
Would be desertion, which I cannot do.'

Then she: 'So helping women in distress,
Is not, as you pretend, a binding thing,
But polite sound that leads to nothingness
When woman's fate some savage choices bring . . .'

43   D

Then Ossian said: 'Princess . . .
We, who serve Finn, are servants of the King,
Your Father . . . what you ask confounds us all.
What you suggest may make the Kingdom fall.

Conan commands us here . . . Will Conan guide?
Is Dermot by his promise bound to go?
It is no petty matter to decide,
But over-fraught with death and overthrow.
In either way, disgrace
And shattering of the order that we know . . .
Not Conan only . . . let a vote go round.'
Then Conan said: 'Dermot is surely bound

To help a suppliant woman when she pleads . . .
But Finn and High-King Cormac put him here,
To guard, and not to go where ruin leads
Because a princess babbles in his ear.
This is our Finn's pledged bride . . .
Grania herself; well, Lady, let us hear
What extreme anguish prompts you to ask this,
And ask of Dermot . . . tell us what it is.'

Then she: 'Harsh Conan, I will answer you . . .
King Cormac now lies drunken in his bed.
When my sweet Mother died, he wed anew
And evil was the woman whom he wed.
He now would marry me
To Finn, than whom I'd rather be struck dead.
Finn, someone thrice my age and drunk as he . . .
That is some reason, since you ask of me.

44

That I choose Dermot calls for no excuse . . .
He comes from oversea: can you suppose
That Finn's own sons are persons I should choose,
Or Ossian's son, or any friends of those?
Which of you here, save he,
Could take me without setting men at blows
And setting blood-feuds going, west and east . . . ?
No vengeance can assail his Kin at least.

Then Conan: 'Lady, I have been Finn's man,
Long years, and now am learned in his ways.
The least forgiving dog since Earth began.
A blood-feud will be candle to the blaze
His taking you will cause.
Finn's vengeance will pursue him all his days,
And Cormac's vengeance, you: I warn you well
You'll die in anguish, having lived in hell.

You, as a Lady, cannot understand
What will result tomorrow when they know.
It is a far cry to your western land,
A weary cry, the way you'll have to go.
You can escape from here
May win a start of twenty miles or so,
Twenty at most; but then, the hue and cry,
With no escape, will hunt you till you die.

Were you ever a hare and hunted by the hounds?
Probably not . . . you swiftly will be, then.
And every King will beat you from his bounds,
From terror of Finn's rage and Cormac's men.

You'll sleep in the wet wood,
Or freeze with the drenched heron in the fen,
And eat the lucky pickings of your theft.
The mouse or fish that fox or otter left.

You will never dare wait dawn where you lay down,
Nor eat where you find food, nor put least trust
In man, woman or child in rath or town.
They'll give you many a curse, but never a crust.
And there you'll stumble on.
Starved, sopping, limping in the mud and dust
And then, the stag-hounds round you, giving tongue,
And you'll be caught, and Dermot will be hung.'

'Come, Conan,' Dermot said, 'we question now
If what the Princess asks me can be done.
If that be voted, I'll consider how.
I ask a yes or no from every one.
Does my oath bind me here,
To help this Princess lovely as the sun,
To get from Tara to her Mother's Kin,
Maugre my oaths to Cormac or to Finn?

You say I must . . . who next, then? Ossian, say.'
'The oath is crazy,' Ossian replied.
'You break with King or Woman either way.
But all Fianna trust the losing side
As needing the help more.
The woman pleads and you must be her guide.'
Then Dermot: 'Two agree . . . will Fand declare?'
'I never heard such nonsense anywhere,'

Fand answered: 'We are henchmen sworn to Finn,
On service here, as Cormac's special guard.
We ate his bread, we have drunken from his bin,
And stay here till the gates are all unbarred.
We are sentries, and must stay
Whatever woman finds the going hard.
To keep this gate for Cormac is our task,
Even if bright Queen Helen come to ask.'

Then Dermot turned to Goll: 'What does Goll say?'
'This,' Goll replied, 'that had she asked us all,
This seven of us, I'd have answered 'Stay . . .
We seven here as sentries on the wall,
As seven must remain.
But since to only one man comes the call,
To Dermot, from a woman in distress,
Dermot must do it: no Knight can do less.'

'Three, for, and one against,' said Dermot. 'Next,
Caoilte; swift-footed Caoilte; what say you?'
' "Fianna men keep promise", is the text,
Keep promise, and give payment before due.
But not when under arms.
When under arms, in army or in crew,
We obey Finn, or Finn's deputed chief,
No matter what complainant come in grief.

Our double-oath is crazy I agree,'
Caoilte added: 'Either way absurd,
And had the lovely lady turned to me,
I would have wakened Finn and said a word.

47

But being asked to vote,
By every kingly law I ever heard,
I say that we and Dermot are the King's,
And stand as such, whatever siren sings.'

'So,' Dermot said, 'two hostile, and three, for . . .
Now, Osgar . . . where is Osgar? he is gone . . .'
Conan and Dermot called him at the door.
In middest night the constellations shone.
'Osgar,' his fellows called.
'Osgar: the captain calls you,' and anon
Osgar came running back and entered in.
He said 'Forgive me . . . I have been to Finn.'

Then, Conan, 'What did Finn say when he heard
His lovebird's sudden impulse to be free?'
'He never woke or understood a word . . .
I shook him, but I had to let him be.
I tried King Cormac next . . .
King Cormac lies as stupefied as he.
Being Finn's grandson, Conan, I made bold
To call the dog, since wolves were in the fold.'

'Well, the dog sleeps; so, Osgar, cast your vote.
Should Dermot take the lady west, or stay?'
'The folly of it almost chokes the throat . . .'
But Dermot's duty is as clear as day,
The suppliant must be helped.
Though crowns are cast and Kingdoms go astray
And honour go dishonoured to the dead.'
'Four for it; two against it,' Dermot said.

48

'Then, Lady, since you plead and votings bid
I will attempt to take you to the west.
My plans for getting westward shall be hid.
I become host and you become my guest.
You and my comrades know,
The folly and the sin are manifest.
Go to your herald's postern and there wait . . .
Tonight's results from tangles of old fate.'

Grania went out, with anger and disdain,
(Yet in a triumph), and the men were mute.
Then, lo, the Princess of the Sun again,
Suddenly with them on a silent foot.
'Ossian,' she said, 'O friends . . .
The evil flower turns to wicked fruit . . .
So rules the trouble of the long ago . . .
And Dermot goes, and Eire's fortunes go.

Alas, Sir Dermot, you will be pursued.
Finn will destroy you and re-take his bride.
But Finn, and all his Knights, will be at feud
And Eire's self their enemy beside.
From the grey Echtge Hills
To Moyle, streaked with its many-tided tide,
Some few of you will totter in your pain,
But only Ossian will know joy again.'

Then Dermot spoke: 'O Lady of Delight,
Destiny deals her unexpected blow,
And fortunes wither as they do tonight.
Ruin must follow, but I have to go.

49

One thing I gladly see,
That in some happy way I cannot know
You in your beauty will bring Ossian peace
In some green garden where all sorrows cease.

But whatsoever fortunes have to be
I shall remember you till fortunes end
And ever thank you that you thought of me.
And now, O Six, think kindly of your friend.
Good-night to you: good-bye.
Whatever human sorrows may impend,
We have shared happy seasons, you and I,
And gifts remain when givers have passed by.

So, Conan, take the ring my father wore,
And Ossian, you, this golden cloak-brooch: Fand,
My hounds at Allan, good at stag or boar.
Caoilte, my stallion from the Eastern land.
Osgar, my Eastern mare.
Goll, the great silver goblets that I took
Raiding the Roman town at Roaring Brook.
I bless you all, soul, body, heart and hand.'

Dismiss me from the watch, Conan.' 'I do,'
Conan replied, 'And none of us will raise
Outcry, or hand, or weapon after you,
Whatever either drunken ruler says.'
The others all agreed.
'It is a far cry to the western ways,'
Said Dermot, pausing at the opened door,
The hinges whimpered as the pintles bore.

He looked his last at them and then was gone,
With quick steps crunching gravel, without word.
Above the door they saw the stars that shone,
The footsteps lapsed and then were no more heard.
The wind had drawn more west
And over Tara, the unlucky bird,
The owl that tells misfortune, came with cry
In long lament for someone soon to die.

PART II

The Breaking of the Fianna
Ossian's Going

Disaster followed fast on the disgrace.
Finn, waking from his drug in early day,
Called for his famous staghounds and gave chase,
Their bell-notes rang along the western way.
'Bring Grania home,' Finn cried,
But if you come on Dermot, never slay . . .
Bring him to me alive, and men shall see
What comes to Body-Guards-Men false to me.'

Grania soon sickened of the hunted life,
Riding and starving, sleeping in the rain;
She rode to Finn, who took her for his wife,
No Body-Guards-Man spoke to her again.
And Dermot Finn beguiled,
Swearing he knew him without spot nor stain,
And evermore would have him as a friend,
Then had him gashed, and mocked him at his end.

All the Fianna brothers' hearts were broken . . .
Finn's Sons and Grandson, all the hearts of gold,
Murmured at Finn, and savage words were spoken,
Till Finn was as a mad dog uncontrolled,
And on bare Burren Edge
His angers struck swift-footed Conan cold,
With all Goll's brothers, beautiful as May,
And Goll died in a cavern by the bay.

Then Eire's Kings cried: 'Let us make an end
Of Finn and all these murderings of Knights.'
They prepared feasts and begged him to attend,
Swearing him peace by many holy rites.
Finn and his Kin believed.
They marched with banners to these false delights.
Three days they feasted, but the treachery then
Made half those trusting feasters murdered men.

Finn, with his best survivors, made a stand
On Gavra Hill, that bitter day, in vain:
For all were killed except a tiny band,
Who struggled north to what might still remain,
Finn's fief, near Tiverà.
Up, under Trostan, in the blinding rain
Sore wounded Osgar, Ossian's princeling, died,
On the lone moorland where the curlews cried.

They heaped a little cairn and left him there.
Then down in the blind rain and the floods roaring
They passed below the red crags beaten bare
Knee deep in water with the breakers warring

They waded a mad stream,
Finn's River from the Hookéd Mountain pouring,
The heather-pasture of the honey bee,
Then halted, on the sea-beach near the sea.

And there, before them, halted fetlock deep
In the sea's wash, that Princess of the Sun
Sat with bowed head to see the heroes weep,
Her stallion mouthed the bubbles as they spun.
A led horse at her side
Whinnied a challenge startling everyone.
The Princess cried aloud: 'O Ossian: friend . . .
Take my love's welcome at your journey's end.

I bring a horse and bid you come with me,
Into a country where Mays never cease
Where wounds are healed and sorrow cannot be
And without ploughing, cornland gives increase,
Where blossom and fruit form
Together in an ecstasy of peace
Where singings never end nor lovers tire,
I, Niamh, bid you, O my heart's desire.'

Even her words seemed to make Ossian young.
He bade his friends farewell with grip of hands.
Sgeolan the staghound whimpered and gave tongue.
Then Ossian crossed the narrow strip of sands.
'Ossian,' we heard her say,
'Mount and away to the Undying Lands . . .
The old things of your sorrow have an end,
Seek new things with undying me for friend.'

He mounted the led stallion of bright eye.
His hand lay upon hers upon the rein,
The horses trod the air into the sky,
Their hoofings sparkled in a fiery lane.
'He is away,' Finn said,
'Eire will never see his like again.'
Onward away the lovers' horses strode.
In the dimmed west the evening planet glowed.

PART III

His coming to the Country of the Young
Ossian tells of his Going

High up, we trod the wind over the isles,
Our stallions striking sparks out of the air,
Ocean lay deep below for many miles
Above, the starry universe lay bare.
Niamh and I alone
Talking or singing, utterly at one,
Gallopped in ecstasies undreamed-of here.
Slowly the darkness became less austere,
The sun was rising and our ride was done,

And heralds gathered, crying 'Niamh, Queen . . .
Be welcome home, dear Lady of Delight . . .
And Ossian, of the bay-leaves ever green,
Be welcome also to undying light.

54

Forget Earth's shadow and storm,
Come to the temple of undying things,
The Order of the priests, the Power of Kings,
And Beauty undying, perfect, infinite.'

O marvellously, the great temple stood,
So exquisitely ordered and arranged
It seemed a mind, not carven stone and wood,
But intellect from every doubt estranged,
And in undying dream.
Beside it, water lapsed over a fall,
And shone in pools along the sunniest wall,
Its wrinkling eddies ever glimpsed and changed.

Above those changing eddies Fortune sat,
Causing Man's lot to prosper or decline,
As Wisdom, the unerring autocrat,
Judged the allotted hour and gave sign.
Her glittering rainbow shone,
As ever-falling water caught the light
The colours were all colours and all bright,
Then dimmed, then seemed to mingle, then were gone.

At Fortune's sign, Niamh made me advance,
I knelt to that dispenser of man's fate,
'Ossian,' she said, 'Your soul's inheritance
Is, to be you, from virtue of old date;
O clay with starry wings;
Here the stream runs, and Order, Beauty and Power
Ask for the Seed-Corn, Fruit, or Matchless Flower,
I, who am Fortune, watch the brook and wait.

Look at the living water of the stream,
It passes and it changes and it grows,
From rain-drops to the turbulent extreme
Wherein the exultant whale his fountain blows
Man is but winter rain.
He hurls out of his tempest into hell;
The beauty of the ocean none can tell.
The order of the ocean no-one knows.

But O, the beauty, the beauty never dying,
Waiting the seeing heart, the doing hand,
The eternities in every instant flying,
The continents unconquered in the sand
The singing in the sky.
The palaces unbuilt, for Kings unborn,
Who yet await the blowing of the horn . . .
That none can find unless he understand.'

Then, singing thus, she turned: Niamh and I
Entered the temple by a little door,
To marvel at the things that cannot die
The souls' adventures worth the venturing for.
'See,' Niamh said, 'they come . . .
These strangers, who have touched this land's extreme
Discovering beauty beyond mortal dream . . .
Listen, the wonder will be acted o'er . . .'

Then on the platform watched by myriad eyes
In the great arc, one, preluding, declared
How one abandoned glory to be wise,
Content with leavings that the lepers shared.

Then, music, as he ceased,
Brought singers, dancers, showing every kind
Of earth's delights that such an one resigned
Then came his very self and how he fared.

O marvellous that wandering up and down
Finding the nothings to which all ways led,
The glory of Hope on entering the town,
The promised gold, achieved, but proven lead.
The seeming wise, so kind,
The daily taunts, embittering the nights,
The jealousies, the treasons and the spites,
The black despair and wishing he were dead.

Then, as I watched, lo, suddenly, the truth
Enlightened him, as it enlightened me:
I was received into the Land of Youth
All understanding, utter ecstasy,
All music, colour, form,
Niamh and I were spirits linked together
With Sun and Stars, the Seasons and the Weather
All moods and modes of life, earth, air and sea.

Niamh and I were one, and all was ours
To know together all the Kingdom held
Of living, without bridle on the powers,
In beauty not yet carven, sung, nor spelled.
Ourselves all young, young, young . . .
As music in a starry dance intense,
In living ecstasy of excellence.
Enchanted and inspired and impelled.

PART IV

The Country of the Young

Into that sunny land our way we took,
Each moment bringing marvel of surprise.
We paused above the well-spring of a brook
Under an elm-tree, on a grassy rise.
The wind-flowers trembled there,
Marvellous flowers, blue and red and white.
'Ossian has come,' they sang, 'to know delight.
Look at us Ossian: Beauty makes men wise.'

Then, from the cressy selvage of the pond,
The tiny frogs, in their wet dwelling trilled
'Niamh and Ossian are in golden bond . . .
They could come swimming, if they only willed,
Into this life so cool,
And hear the eel-fish telling of the Sea,
A stranger pond where many marvels be,
A great deep hollow, with salt water filled.'

Upon the budded branchings of a thorn,
A blackbird sang, 'O Ossian, you and I
Are of the happiest creatures ever born;
We sit in sun and see the Spring go by.
Within our minds a Sun
Bids us to sing of love in the green wood,
For Spring, and Love, and Singing are all good:
They give the earth the glory of the sky.'

The seven spirits of that April land
Floated together singing to our feet,
The leader bearing brooklime in her hand,
One, scarlet hips, one, ears of ripened wheat,
One, clover, red and white,
One, the white violets, sweeter than first love,
One, harebells blue as any sky above,
One, just the green grass that the horses eat.

'Ossian,' they sang, 'look at these lovely things,
Look closely.' So I looked, and I perceived,
The marvel of the rootlets' tiny strings
That work the magic not to be believed.
To draw from the raw clay
The unseen tiny nothings that yet make
(Untaught) a beauty for the beauty's sake
In the many-flowered marvel million-leaved.

O ecstasy on ecstasy that thrilled
That timeless time, to understand the seeds
Unseen within the dark, that yet can build
Woman for beauty, or a man for deeds.
Knowledge ran like the light
Running across a field when clouds are driven,
Ran in my mind, like coming-in of Heaven,
And Niamh sang like the murmuring of reeds.

'Ossian,' she sang, 'Beloved; follow me . . .
Learn that the growing-place is very vast . . .
For, though the land be bounded by the sea,
And many journeys have been over-past,

Yet still, beyond, beyond,
There are the singing circles of great awe,
The beauty like a planet giving law
To new life sprung from our imagined last.'

Then, at her touch, we were among the snows,
The basalt powdered frosty, the green ice,
Piled where the iceberg from the glacier goes,
With scarified gripped granites in its vice.
Eternal silence there,
Save, when, at iron times a clangor claps
As in the floe another chasm snaps,
Or too intense a midnight splits the gneiss.

Yet, at another touch, we were away,
In forests seemingly without an end,
Unshedded green-ness in eternal sway,
Eternal murmur, friend to giant friend,
In language of old time,
Repeating memories forever hid
Of what the dragon and the mammoth did
Ere conquering man had any life to spend.

We saw the manless sands under the sun,
The grass-lands pasturing their multitude,
The rivers where un-numbered salmon run,
And then a hill-top where a city stood
With weather-cocks of gold.
That gleamed like fire as they turned and cried
'Ossian has come among us with his bride.
O welcome them into the Brotherhood!'

They bade us welcome at the city gate,
No evil in that city can endure.
All lovely things, all things of good report
Crown all its towers, make all its bases sure.
'O marvellous,' I cried.
'This is the city of our dreams of old,
The city in the west, as travellers told,
Where the well of living wisdom gushes pure.'

And there, again, the citizens were friends.
So wise they were that many a timeless day
We talked a glorious question to its ends
Till all but ecstasy was put away.
Each lovely mind had light
Not only to illumine the theme conned
But show the landscape of the thoughts beyond
Where the spirits of the stars made holiday.

How long we tarried in that splendid place
I cannot tell, so tense each second seemed,
Each man so wise, each woman of such grace,
Each meeting perfect beyond all things dreamed.
But one day, a day dawned,
With leaden haze unlike a morning there,
My lovely Niamh was not anywhere . . .
No friends, no city, only earth that steamed.

It was not steam, but smoke, darkening earth,
And then strange figures with a stallion came;
They bitted him, they buckled-in the girth,
Then turned to me and called me by my name.

'Ossian, you Son of Finn,
See now the desert where the fire burns . . .
This is the borderland of no returns:
You have one moment: mount and ride the flame.

I had no moment, for the fire was there,
The men gone, the horse shying, the smoke dense,
With whirls of burning fragments in the air
I reached the saddle as he bounded thence.
Flame was all round me, roaring;
Nothing but fire seemed to be the world.
Into its midst with scorching hair we hurled
I gallopped amid fire without sense.

At last, I fell; and lay; and then, a gate,
A city-gate and wall, lofty and barred,
Where solitude in silence held her state
And no least swallow's cry the quiet marred.
All fire was gone: white cloud
Lay at my feet: the city-gates immense
Moved slowly open: Niamh issued thence.
'Welcome,' she said: 'Friend, was the riding hard?'

She took my hand and led me through the gates
Into a town of palaces and towers
Built by the spirit's triumph over fates,
The things eternal won from bitter hours,
Things that death cannot touch.
Man's divine moods had made that city fair,
Temple and monument and city-square.
The city and its treasures, all were ours.

In a lily-garden where the fountains shone
I gazed, I marvelled, and I understood
Its glory from the burning undergone.
'This is the Place of man's beatitude . . .
O loveliest Niamh, tell . . .
Why should a rag like me, a rat that dies,
Be with you thus within this Paradise
O starry spirit, cloaked in womanhood,

Why should you bless me, and who are you . . . Tell.'
'I am your Helper stablished from of old,
So the bright balances of Fortune fell
So the all-seeing destinies foretold . . .
And this, my dwelling-place,
This is the City built in Beauty's praise
By deathless beings in forgotten days
Who sought the sunlight in the bitter cold.'

Out of the garden's joy a music rose
Like muted strings, or breath where nothing grieved,
An ecstasy of unity with those
Who sought the living sunlight and achieved.
Slowly the music swelled
Then from its murmur human voices sang
Lifting aloft until the City rang
'Beauty endures where Wisdom has believed.'

I cannot guess what generations passed
In the dear daylight of that deathless place,
But sunset reddened and light dimmed at last
And shadows crept to darken and efface.

But in one tower, a light
Showed that a Something watched if others slept,
Then, in the dimness leaves of brightness swept
Like fire-flies or bats that left no trace.

What could they be, these little wandering flames,
Floating like leaves, or like bats beating by,
Will-driven some, or one with the wind's aims,
Tossed often into whirls and lifted high.
They gleamed and disappeared.
What could they be, for as they glittered near
They seemed to whisper what I could not hear
And as I did not heed they seemed to sigh?

'Niamh,' I said, 'for pity, tell me, then,
What are these leaves that seem intent to speak?'
'They are the prayings of the souls alive
Crying in anguish for the peace they seek.
This is where prayings come . . .
Would you, then, look at whence these prayings rise.
You are advanced, you have inhuman eyes,
You can now help, you are no longer weak.

Look, then, below.'
                    I looked, and lo, a rath,
A hill-town, burning, smoking to the sky,
The reivers beating cattle down the path,
The spearmen storming with the battle-cry,
The warders dead in flame,
Survivors crying 'Help', where no help was,
Knowing that final Fate had come to pass,
The young to be enslaved, the old to die.

'Look, then, again' . . .

             And lo, a city sick
With unknown pestilence, her people dying,
The death-pits heaped with victims, some still quick,
Women and children in the gutters lying.
Children, with none to tend
Wailing, or being beaten by the guards,
Who sat at bonfires, drunken, playing cards.
Outside, the country-people killed the flying.

'Look, then, again' . . .

             and lo, the women's lives,
The desolated ones whose day was past,
The broken-hearted ones, the widowed wives,
Those with dead children, childless and aghast . . .
And then, beyond all these
All the bewildered misery of the ache
Of folly and frustration and mistake
Before the life's one happy breath, the last . . .

Then, lo, an Irish voice the silence broke
A singing from amidst those wandering fires . . .
Singing a sudden song that made me choke,
My song of Spring and lovely Spring's desires,
The song I made of old
Of May in Antrim happy ages since;
Of blossom on the hawthorn, and the quince,
When cuckoos come and lambs are in the byres.

Then, at the song's end, came a poet's cry
The cry of youth that loves the spirit's flower,
And follows seeking beauty till he die,
Seeking in bitter anguish for the power
So very seldom won.
And this man prayed to me, whose strivings seemed
So paltry to the glories I had dreamed;
He prayed to me in his despairing hour.

'O, Ossian, help me to attain, like you,
The power to evoke in mortal minds
The quiet at the dropping of the dew;
The belling of the red stags for the hinds
On Trostan of the mists;
The hint of what it is that curlews cry,
Laughter or grief above us, going by,
Laughter that tears the heart, or grief that blinds.

O, teach me, Ossian, for I long and long
To serve that Power and attain the skill,
To put my heart's desire in a song
And leave words living when my heart is still,
Words, only words, that yet
Kindle the startling image that persists,
The sorrow of the moorland in the mists,
The singing of the skylarks on the hill.'

Alas, that cry out of the passing flame,
That memory of curlews overhead . . .
Was Finn's beloved Allan still the same?
Were gannets plunging beyond Garron Head?

And O was lovely Saeve
My Mother, whom, for many a bitter year,
Druids bewitched into a wandering deer
Hunted by hounds, was she alive or dead?

And, instantly, it seemed, beneath me lay
The Earth, the migrant bird-flocks of the Spring,
The wild-geese of the world upon their way
In cry like hounds and thundering on the wing.
And O, desire smote hard,
To watch with the Fianna as they went
Ere April brings the colour and the scent
But the grass pushes and the robins sing.

'Niamh,' I cried, 'my kindred linger there . . .
I must away among the birds to know
Finn once again, forgetting faults that were;
And all those friends in whom I gloried so,
The war-worn Holy Band . . .
'O spirits of the wilderness,' I cried
'Carry me with you on your running tide,
Take me to Eire with you as you go.'

But Niamh was not there to answer me;
The time had fallen and the change begun;
The geese were flying with me over sea;
Dark on the waves I saw our shadows run
As the great roaring sped.
Above all winds my carriers swept the skies,
Thunder and swerve, great purpose, staring eyes,
A myriad madness utterly at one.

Till, lo, the Hookéd Hill and Tiverà,
Finn's fief, the mountain dairy and the ling,
The river with the pools where salmon are . . .
Yes, and the fowlers crouched with bow and sling,
Watching the homing birds.
I felt the geese swerve as the missiles flew,
I fell on the beloved land I knew,
Fell into age, an old, bent, broken thing.

Suddenly round me were the fowlers' hands,
Men with odd speech, odd clothing, with new ways;
I saw new buildings on Finn's dairy lands,
With cows of unknown breeding out at graze,
All gone were the grey geese.
No Niamh showed: and I, all old and bent
A worn-out coin, too battered to be spent,
Shaken, in sorrow, sick, and in a daze.

Then there were bells, and then a great man stood
Asking if I were hurt? I asked for Finn,
Finn, or some comrade of the Brotherhood.
He said 'Wait, Brother, till we bear you in . . .
How was this poor soul hurt?'
They said 'The geese came over, giving tongue,
He must have caught the pebble someone slung . . .
And here we found him lying in the whin.'

They bore me to a bed and laid me there.
The great man tended me and made me rest.
Another life breathing another air
Commanded Eire: this was manifest.

A greater life than mine . . .
But I, who longed for Niamh once again
Even one bitter glimpse in winter rain
Would have been balm to make all better best.

'Friend, I am Patrick,' thus the great man spoke:
'And you?' I told him: 'Ossian, son of Finn,
The High King's Captain, till the Kingdom broke.
Ask him to come, or others of my Kin . . .
Finn, who commands this glen . . .'
'Friend, Finn was dead and buried centuries since.
And Ossian disappeared, that famous prince.
Their house is roof-less: no-one dwells therein.'

'Then, Niamh, my Beloved, where is she?
Niamh, with whom I was away, away,
In the sun land, in the star land, over sea . . .
Early today . . . or was it yesterday? . . .
The green undying land . . .'
'Friend, the tales tell, that centuries ago,
That Lady came for Ossian there below;
They rode into the clouds at Garron Bay.'

'Yes . . . so it was. Where is she? Is she here?'
'No,' Patrick said, 'the people tell the tale . . .
With other tales of wonder and of fear,
But this is Finn's old fief and dairy-vale,
Where his last Kinsmen died,
Two centuries ago, before our Spring,
Our Easter Primrose blossomed in the King
And those old warrior times began to fail.

But you are Ossian: we have often heard
Your poems; they are well-remembered still . . .
The apple-blossom and the cuckoo bird
And the curlews laughing on the Hookéd Hill . . .
Drink this, then sleep awhile . . .
Then, when refreshed, let all my lads attend . . .
We should account it more than honour, friend,
To hear you sing your poems, if you will . . .'

Then I, unhappy, broken, agéd, lone,
Feeling all lost, unreal, evil, dim,
My every muscle aching on the bone,
My every beauty withered on the limb,
Seeing this man so great,
So beautiful and kind to one so lost,
The bitter river of my death was crossed.
'I will most gladly sing,' I answered him.

PART V

Of the Death and Burial of Ossian

I, who was Patrick's Novice, tell the rest:
While tending Ossian he bade me bring
A harp and catgut from the music chest,
But could not turn the peg to stretch the string.
'I am so weak . . . so weak' . . .
He said, 'I cannot: so forgive me, friend,
All music comes to silence at the end.
I was the Bard, when Cormac was the King.'

He could not sing that day, nor the next day,
But talked with Patrick, who consoled and cheered.
Then after sunrise, rousing where he lay,
He cried 'To each, according to his weird . . .
Sorrow, Love, Glory, Death.
O holy, glorious Patrick, call your men,
I look my last upon my Father's glen.
I call upon the Star by which I steered.'

He looked towards the east, where the tracks cross;
St Patrick propped him up, the doors lay wide;
Then Ossian said: 'I see the banners toss,
The stallions of the stars are in their pride . . .
Surely, she comes, she comes . . .
O well-beloved beauty, be again
My taker from an agony of pain,
I am a dying dust, but you abide.

O take me once again out of the woe,
Into the wonder that at each point won
Reveals more wonder beautiful to know,
Another deed more splendid to be done.
Guide me once more away . . .
O bright Fianna stepping to the fife,
Ossian is dusty with the rags of life
I long for Niamh, Princess of the Sun.'

And lo, as his voice faltered and was still,
He, looking eastward, startled, and exclaimed . . .
'Niamh . . . my Niamh, coming down the hill . . .
And, truly, there, a shining Knighthood flamed,
White-horsed, with banners bright.

71

They halted where the ragwort always grows,
And there a woman lovelier than a rose
Held a white stallion saddled but untamed.

She left the horses there: she neared the doors
And Ossian cried 'My Niamh ... it is she ...'
And lo, like pure gold won from molten ores,
We saw his spirit let his ruins be ...
His soul, the green earth's pride,
Rose from the tattered figure on the bed,
That drooped collapsed upon the pillow, dead,
And Niamh spoke 'My Ossian ... come with me.'

And there they passed together into air
In sparkles, eastward: we, as Patrick bade,
Made ready the worn husk for burial there:
Logs, gorses, peats and slivered yews we laid
Around the chieftain's bed.
Over the standing stones we built the pyre,
Then singing Christian hymns we lit the fire,
The great bones burned to ashes as we prayed.

EIGHTY-FIVE TO WIN

England's Second Innings
against
The Australian Eleven
at
Kennington Oval
on
Tuesday, 29 August 1882

THE AUSTRALIAN ELEVEN	THE ENGLISH ELEVEN
A. C. Bannerman	R. G. Barlow
H. H. Massie	Dr W. G. Grace
W. L. Murdoch (*Captain*)	G. Ulyett
G. J. Bonnor	A. P. Lucas
T. Horan	Hon. A. Lyttelton
G. Giffen	C. T. Studd
J. McC. Blackham	J. M. Read
T. W. Garrett	W. Barnes
H. F. Boyle	A. G. Steel
S. P. Jones	A. N. Hornby (*Captain*)
F. R. Spofforth	E. Peate

Though wayward Time be changeful as Man's will,
We have the game, we have the Oval still,
And still the Gas-Works mark the Gas-Works End
And still our sun shines and the rains descend.

Speak to me, Muse, and tell me of the game
When Murdoch's great Eleven overcame.

73

Laurels were tensely lost and hardly won
In that wild afternoon at Kennington,
When more than twenty thousand watchers stared
And cheered, and hoped, and anguished, and despaired.

Tell of the Day, how heavy rain had cleared
To sunshine and mad wind as noon-time neared,
Then showers (sometimes hail) on strong blasts cold,
Making a wicket good for men who bowled.
Such was the Day, when England's side went in
Just before four, with eighty-five to win.

Grace, and the Captain (Hornby), led the way,
(Grace to face Spofforth) in beginning play.
Spofforth was bowling from the Gas-Works End,
Garrett across.
                The opposites contend.

What was this Spofforth, called The Demon yet,
For men forget, but cannot all forget?
A tall, lean, wiry athlete inly lit
With mind, and saturnine control of it.
Is it not said, that he, with either hand,
Could fling a hen's egg, onto grass or sand,
Clear seventy yards, yet never crack the shell?

Then, when he bowled, he seemed a thing of Hell,
Writhing; grimacing; batsmen, catching breath,
Thought him no mortal man but very Death;
For no man ever knew what ball would come
From that wild whirl, save one from devildom.

74

Now the sharp fears came tugging at the heart,
As Cunning strove with Care and Skill with Art.

Hornby and Grace, with eighty-five to win,
Watched for some balls, then made the runs begin.

Ten had gone up, when Hornby's wicket went
(His off-stump), from a ball that Spofforth sent.
One, for fifteen; and Barlow took his place.
Barlow, our safest bat, came in with Grace:
Barlow, the wonder, famed in song and story,
The Red Rose County's well-remembered glory.
The first ball Spofforth sent him bowled him clean.
Two gone, of England's surest, for fifteen.

But Grace alone was power manifest,
(Of all men there, he is remembered best)
The great, black-bearded Doctor, watchful-eyed,
Next to our Queen, that vanished England's pride;
Grace was still in; and Ulyett joined him there.

Slowly the scoring mounted from the pair.
To Twenty, Thirty, Forty, and anon
Garrett was taken off and Boyle put on
And Spofforth changed to the Pavilion End.

Thirty odd runs and seven bats to spend,
Surely a task so simple could be done?
Ulyett and Grace seemed settled and at one.

F

Fifty went up, and then a marvel came,
Still something told by lovers of the game.
Spofforth sent down a ball that Ulyett hit,
No barest chance (it seemed) to mortal wit.
Snicked, high and wide it went, yet with one hand,
Blackham just caught it and dissolved the stand.
Three gone, for fifty-one.

              Lucas joined Grace,
Two partners famed in many a happy case,
But not, alas, for then, for two runs more,
Grace was caught out, at fifty-three for four,
Caught from a ball by Boyle, for Boyle had found
All he could wish in that uncertain ground.

Still thirty-two to win, with six to fall,
Lyttelton joined, and brought delight to all,
Enchanting promise came, for runs were scored,
Lucas and he put sixty on the board.
And then the conflict quieted to grim.

For master-spirits shine when hopes are dim;
Australia's best, all at their best, were there.
Light, wicket, and themselves, all bade beware.
The field were all lithe leopards on the pounce:
Each ball had a new break at every bounce.

Twelve deadly overs followed without score.
Then came a run, then deadly maidens more.
Then Spofforth shattered Destiny's arrest
And Lyttelton's mid-stump was scattered west.

Five gone, for sixty-six, but Hope, still green,
Felt, the last five would make the last nineteen.
Had we not Steel, and Studd, and Maurice Read,
Three superb bats? how could we fail to speed?
Here, Hornby, saving a reserve to win,
Re-made the order of the going-in,
Putting in Steel, not Studd, at fifth man gone,
Thinking that Studd might save us later on,
If any later on might need a stay.

A strain and anguish settled on the day,
As Steel came in; but Lucas cut a four;
Not nineteen now but only fifteen more.

Steel hit his first ball back to Spofforth's hand.

Then Maurice Read gave centre and took stand . . .

Read, Surrey's pride, who ever made hope thrill
In doubtful games when things were going ill.
If Read could stay . . .
                        But Spofforth's second ball
Made the mid-stump of Surrey's pride to fall.
Seven men out, and fifteen still to get.

But William Barnes was never careless yet;
A watchful batsman he, though skilled to smite,
Barnes joined with Lucas in the doubtful fight.

Wild was the cheerless weather, wild the light,
Wild the contesting souls whom Hope had fired.

All the Australian team were men inspired,
Spofforth had said the matter 'could be done',
And all the live eleven were as one.
The Hope was theirs, the Hope that ever wins,
The Hope that sways the tossed coin as it spins,
The starry Hope that ever makes man learn
That to the man who Hopes the luck will turn.
The twenty-two at bay were face to face.

The watchers' hearts stood still about the place.

In risk so hateful, hoping so intense,
One English watcher died there, of suspense.

Barnes hit a two; three lucky byes were run;
Ten more to win, what joy to everyone.
All cheered for every run and faces shone,
Then Lucas played a ball of Spofforth's on.
Eight, of ten, out, and seventy-five the score.
'Over' was called: the fieldsmen loitered o'er.

They paused in little groups to mutter low
The secret hints the bats were not to know.
Then, watching Studd, they tautened, each in place.
Studd, our reserve, acclaimed a second Grace.

Studd stood at watch by Boyle, the Gas-Works End;
On Boyle and Barnes the minute's issues pend.

The ball had come to Boyle, who paused awhile,
To give it hand-hold in the sawdust-pile,
Then walked, intent, and as he turned to run,
Saw twenty thousand faces blurred to one,
And saw, ahead, a great bat tensely wait
The ball he held, the undelivered Fate.

He ran, he bowled, his length ball took its flight
Down the drear wicket in uncertain light,
It lifted, struck on Barnes's glove, and leapt
To Murdoch, watching point, who caught, and kept.
Nine gone, for seventy-five, and last man in.
Just nine more runs to tie, and ten to win.

Peate, Yorkshire's bowler, came in Barnes's place.
The last man in, with three more balls to face.
Could he but stand until Boyle's over ended,
Stand, keeping in, then all might be amended.
The other end would bat, and Studd was there;
Studd, Cambridge Studd, the bright bat debonair.
A prayer to Peate went up from England's sons:
'Keep steady, Yorkshire, Studd will get the runs.
You, who throughout the game have done so much . . .
Now, stand . . . keep in . . . put nothing to the touch.'

Peate took his stand: Boyle bowled his second ball.

A tumult of glad shouting broke from all,
Peate smote it lustily to leg, for two.

The ball returned and Boyle began anew.

Seven to tie, and eight to win the game.

Boyle launched another, subtly not the same;
And half the white-faced watchers, staring tense,
Bit their umbrella handles in suspense.

The third ball came, but like a deedless day
It passed unhit, and ceased to be in play.

An instant's respite: only one more ball
And Studd will play, unless Peate's wicket fall.

Boyle took the ball; he turned; he ran; he bowled,
All England's watching heart was stricken cold.

Peate's whirling bat met nothing in its sweep.
The ball put all his wickets in a heap;
All out, with Studd untried; our star had set,
All England out, with seven runs to get.

The crowd sat stunned an instant at the blow,
Then cheered (and none had heard men cheering so),
Cheered the great cricket that had won the game.

In flood onto the pitch the watchers came,
Spofforth and Boyle were lifted shoulder high.

Brief, brief, the glow, even of Victory.
Man's memory is but a moment green.
Chronicle now the actors in the scene,
Unmentioned yet, as Massie, who had made
Life-giving runs, with Bannerman to aid;

Jones, Giffen, Bonnor, Horan, all who shared
Those deadly hours when disaster stared.

Quickly the crowd dispersed to life's routine
Of Life and Death and wonder what they mean.
A thunder muttered and a shower fell
As twilight came with star and Vesper-bell.
Over the Oval, stamped where Spofforth bowled,
Reviving grass-blades lifted from the mould.

ODYSSEUS TELLS

Tell of the Wooden Horse that ruined Troy?

I'll tell you of the Horse, but Destiny,
The Fate that none escapes from, ruined Troy.

What was Troy like? A fortress on a hill,
Windy, wide-wayed, well-walled and wonderful.
With two great temples and King Priam's palace,
Above a grass plain marvellous for horses.
There are no such horses now, nor such a City.

What brought the Greeks to Troy? Not what men say.

King Agamemnon's greed, envy and hate
Of ought more wealthy and splendid than himself.

He forced us there, that godless King of ours,
Hoping for easy conquest and great plunder.

What with that idiot King and pestilence,
We were beaten before Troy, and three parts starved;
In mutiny, on brink of anarchy,
And winter coming: friends, in two weeks more
Any Greek man would have killed any King
Who tried to keep him there besieging Troy.

The King knew clearly what I thought of him,
But someone had to tell him how things stood.
And so I spoke . . .
                    If I had held my peace
The Greeks would have cut Agamemnon's throat,
And sailed for home and Troy would still be Troy.

But, no, I spoke, and as I spoke, a Captain
Brought news that young Prince Ilus, Priam's son,
His youngest son, consecrate to Apollo,
Had just been captured by our foragers,
And Agamemnon said 'Let the young dog
Be branded, and then sold to slavery.'

Then I was fool enough to speak again.
'O Majesty,' I said, 'This is a chance
Of making peace with honour to both sides.
A chance that the gods send to end the war.
The Prince must be returned: he is Apollo's.
We should insult Apollo, shaming him,
And outrage to Apollo brings swift death.
Send him, with all our captives, back to Troy.
You could demand Queen Helen in exchange,
But add some gifts: King Priam loves his son.
He will accept such terms, or any terms.'

What, do you think, the sulky dog replied?
'Not thus do Argive Kings commanding armies
Treat with insulting foes. Dismiss, the Council.'

This, to pure sense, when, without sudden peace,
The army meant to kill him and go home.

Well, after we had gone, the ruffian saw
At least, the risk of outraging Apollo.
He had had enough of that, not long before . . .

A herald went to Troy that afternoon.

Then, there came truce, 'for burying the dead'.
Then, there came friendliness, while young Prince Ilus
Went home to Troy with gifts, paying no ransom,
With all our other Trojan prisoners,
(All not yet sold as slaves) all ransomless.

Then there came generosity from Priam,
A great heart greatly touched by generous deeds;
Not only wine, oil, meat and barley meal,
But all the Greeks made prisoners of war,
All, since the trouble started, without ransom.

Some of those men had been in Troy for years,
Some, from before the war, merchants from Argos,
Subjects of Menelaus and our King,
By no means glad to be restored to them.

There were three of these . . . I saw them coming in
From Troy, each laden with especial gifts.
I saw how terrified they were to come.
They flung themselves at Agamemnon's feet
Laying their gifts before him, gold, gems, spice.
The King looked on them with contempt, and said,
'Take these for further question to my quarters.'

Then, as the three were taken by the guards,
He kicked their gifts to Menelaus, saying,
'Dowry for your recovered Helen, brother.'
And followed, snarling, underneath his breath.

Within the hour, he was back again;
And secret as he was, some inner joy
Was moving his black spirit wickedly.
He said 'I must send instantly to Priam.
Call in the Herald . . . Brother, our Star rises.'

What the dog meant I had not the least guess,
Except that something evil gladdened him.
But the Herald went to Troy with olive sprays,
Asking for armistice 'for propitiation
For desecration of Apollo's pastures.'
(The green plain outside Troy; our battlefield.)

Within an hour Apollo's Priest from Troy
Came, saying this, 'Apollo's Oracle,
Speaking the God's will through His Prophetess,
Bids Greece and Troy cease war till the new moon.
At new moon, let them meet outside Troy gate,
Pour a libation of new wine and swear
A lasting peace, made binding with rich gifts.'

Well . . . that was Peace, at least until new moon.
Most certain peace, forever, as I thought.

I did not see the King, but heard report
That secretly amid the Argos ships
He was preparing a great sacred peace gift.

The time went by: the day of New Moon came.

Suddenly Agamemnon sent for me
(By armed guard). There they sat, he and his brother,
Inside that secret hut, beside a vast
Fierce wooden stallion skinned with beaten gold.
'Come here,' the King said, 'and swear secrecy.'
I swore, expecting evil; then he said:

'This Horse you look at is our gift to Troy.
It will be dragged to Troy this afternoon,
While we swear peace with Priam as arranged.
It will be left there while we burn our camp,
And sail for home according to the order.

When our camp burns and the Greek ships have sailed,
The Trojans are to drag this votive Horse
Up to Apollo's temple in the city.
As offering to Apollo when day dawns.

Listen . . . within the Horse will be five men.
You, who know Troy so well, command the party.
My Brother will be second, under you.
The third, Epeios here, who made the Horse,
The others here, in blood-feud against Troy.

You five will go within the Horse at once;
You will have air enough: you will keep silence
Whatever happens: if you but keep silence
No man can possibly suspect the guile.

86

When the cocks crow in Troy tomorrow morning
Then you, as Captain will undo the bolts,
Creep out, with all the Four, to the South Gate,
Strangle the sentry and unbar the gate.

Three hundred picked men of the army here,
Will not have sailed for home, but come ashore,
Marched in the night to Troy, and will be there,
To enter and take Troy as the gate opens.

We do not ask your comment, but put trust
In your wise judgment. When our plan succeeds
Be sure, the Throne of Argos will be grateful.

Now practise in the Horse: within the hour
You Five will be within it, bound for Troy,
Troy will be ours before morning dawns.'

We practised in the Horse: entering, leaving,
Trying the bolts, amazed at the thing's craft.
That wooden stallion was a masterpiece.
We sharpened up our knives: we ate and drank,
And took a bowl of grapes for sustenance.
Then, it was time; and as I entered last,
And saw the gleam on Agamemnon's face,
My many first misgivings became blacker.
And as I drew the bolts that shut us in
I thought of what a madman once had said:
'He who wants anything unspeakably,
Must sacrifice his nearest, dearest, wisest,
Staunchest, nay, very manhood, for success,
Then will succeed, and then, repent the cost.'

Were we five Agamemnon's sacrifice?

But we were under way, dragged by six horse-teams,

There, in that sweltering Horse, I could reflect,
On Agamemnon's blackest treachery,
This devilry of his to god and man.

There, outside Troy, we heard him swear to Priam
A lasting peace by earth, air, sun and moon.

I shuddered lest the gods should smite us dead.

The ritual ceased . . . then Agamemnon cried
'Priam, our Brother, the Greeks sail for home,
Leaving this Horse of peace as pledge of peace.'

Priam replied, 'May the gods bless our peace.'
The parties moved away, leaving us there.

The sun had set: our stifling den was cooler,
Outside, some Trojan allies marched from Troy.
Quite close, above us, people on Troy walls
Talked as they watched for something, then a rider
Came galloping to Troy from the sea beach.
'They've put to sea, King Priam,' the rider cried,
'They've fired their camp; it is blazing end to end.'

I had guessed as much from cheering on the walls.
These were the signs of peace they had awaited.

88

Now came the test: could Priam be so mad,
Could any living mortal be so mad,
As to believe King Agamemnon's oath?
Could great Apollo's priests and prophetess
Drag such a Plot of Death to the God's House
(Or into Troy) unwarned by the God's self?
If King or Priest were blind, surely some Trojan
Would cause our Horse to stay outside the walls?

Friends, King and Priest and Trojan were at one
In saying that this Argive offering,
This consecration of enduring peace,
Should enter Troy dragged by the votaries
Of that great grey-eyed Queen to Whose live Wisdom
I was from youth sworn servant consecrate.

I heard Her servants, from Her sacred House,
Her Trojan House, the holiest place on Earth,
Singing Her Hymn, come to us from the Gate
To bring us into Troy, to ruin Troy.

I bit my knuckles in my agony.
This was why Agamemnon made me Captain
That all the infamy of sacrilege
Should rest on me, that so I might be burned.

The singers manned the ropes and dragged us in,
Still singing, into Troy, up the paved way,
Through a great crowd into the central square,
Outside Apollo's Temple, where they stopped.

We were in Troy: and now, friends, Life or Death?

Life, seemingly: the High Priest told the crowd
That this great Gift was fashioned for Apollo;
That it should rest in quiet till tomorrow,
Then dragged away and burned at the God's spring.
'It is the God's Horse, bringing peace; keep peace;
And thank the undying Gods for giving peace.'

Well . . . the crowd shuffled round and stared and went,
There was a guard about us all the time
Telling folk not to touch God's holy Horse.
But presently, when there were fewer guards,
A noisier rabble gathered, calling 'Fire.
Bring fire, we will burn the image here . . .
'Yes, burn it now.' They cursed: they struck the Horse.
I thought 'This is the end: we must escape.'

And just as I laid hand upon the bolts
Ready to let us out . . . a something came
That checked the rage and made our blood run cold.

It was a laughter forced from too much grief.
It was King Priam's daughter, mad Kassandra.

She cried, 'I am Kassandra, Apollo's priestess.
He is all Light, all Fire, and I am His,
Or shall be soon.
                    In the green Idan field
Among the daffodils, he courted me.
We could have gone into the living Spring
He *was* the Living Spring – but, no, I could not.

Again, in bluebell time, with apple-blossom,
Like living Summer, Apollo begged my love . . .
We could have entered Summer side by side,
Undying Summer, whose swallows never fly.
I would not though; a girl is a shy thing.

But I was wrong to refuse, for my love burns,
I, being now Apollo, I burn, I burn,
With the inmost truth that nobody believes.

Apollo will woo again before the snow falls.

What is this false Horse that you call Apollo's?

Apollo has his horses in the wild . . .
Stallions on Ida: dolphins in the sea . . .
This is no Horse.
     Listen . . . Are you a Horse?
He says 'I am a little house of death.'

Who made you, then, to be a house of death?
He says 'King Menelaus paid for me,
The master craftsmen made me, and their thought
Is blood and running death and running fire
That will never cease, for Troy will burn forever,
Over her murdered dead.
     These towers will glow
Forever red under the blackest cloud
Of any funeral pyre.'
    The Horse says this'

Then, in the utter silence, Priam's voice.
'Come, little Daughter; it is late and dark,
The god Apollo bids all mortals sleep.
Even his servants have to sleep . . . and you . . .
Come, now, away to rest; this way, with me.'

Steps died away . . . the muttering crowd dispersed,
But guard was set; a dozen guards at least,
They stayed: and we, within the Horse, we, too,
Stayed, cramped, half-frozen now, and stupefied.

I, who commanded, had to face the fact . . .
The time was not yet midnight: cocks would crow
A long sea-watch ahead; and these new guards
Would stay till dawn, or till a guard relieved.

Well . . . could we five endure five hours more?

I doubted it: we were in torment there.

But if I opened-up, surprised the sentries,
In sudden dark attack, we might escape.
If not, when we attempted this at dawn
We should be all too stiff with cramp to struggle.

I muttered to myself 'The worst of evil
Is, always, just the fear of it. Endure.'

After a weary while the guard was changed
The new guard ate and drank and settled down.

And hours passed, for hours always pass.
The burning summers pass and the rains come,
The killing winters pass and the leaves come.
I thought 'Tonight will pass and cocks will crow.'
Our guardsmen seemed to sleep: Troy seemed to sleep,
Even we slept at last; a sort of sleep.

Then suddenly with scream after shrill scream,
Cries, movement, rushing feet, Kassandra came,
She had some pan of fire, for I saw light.
'Fire, fire,' she cried, 'Apollo bids me fire,
This sepulchre of hell, this pod of death
Before its seeds spread fire and death in Troy.'

She struck the Horse with a great pan of fire
Again, again, again, screaming out 'Fire'.

All the guards roused, and women came with lights,
And all there tried to seize this god-possessed
Wild prophetess in frenzy, but she flung free.

Priam and Hecuba came hurrying-in.

Mind you, the coals had set the Horse on fire,
The mane had burnt; the fire had been scattered
And things were singeing: the Horse was full of smoke,
There was a crowd about us; Kassandra fighting,
People beating or treading out the fire,
And Kassandra, quelled, flung sobbing upon the floor,
Priam and Hecuba were tender to her,
They helped her to a seat where she sat moaning,
Men bringing water splashed it on the Horse.

Suddenly, Kassandra clasped the Horse and spoke..
'Menelaus, and Epeios and Odysseus . . .
And two men, red with blood, thirsting for blood.
We burnt your city, long ages ago,
You have forgotten where; I have forgotten;
But the all-living justice never forgets.
You come to burn our city, fire for fire . . .
Another long long agony, repenting.

O friends, go to your rest, but before sleep,
Pray to Apollo, to be merciful
To this His city, whose stallion saved his Mother.
You Greeks, whose sea-horse saved His Mother, pray,
Pray, too, before the fires within you win.

I will go pray, for quiet comes to me . . .
After the mad seas of the storm, the swell,
The slow, dim heave, exhaustion, seeking rest.'

Deep silence fell, then Priam ordered 'Go',
To all folk there: then, gently, 'Come, Kassandra.'

The lights moved with the footsteps, east and west.
The lights and footsteps died: we were alone.
Alone in Troy, past midnight, in silent Troy.

Then, instantly, I whispered, 'Out; now; out.'
I drew the bolt . . . somehow, we all crawled out.
Choked with the smoke, spent, aching, agonised.
They were for lying prone: I, who knew Troy,
Cursed them for mutineers. 'Come, hide,' I hissed.

King Menelaus called me: 'Insolent dog.'
'Dog, sir, yourself,' I said, 'I command here.
Get, all of you, within that temple door.
In, now; in, all of you: in, all of you.'

So, what with oaths and blows I drove them in,
Into the secret space behind the altar.
There we could stretch, O joy untellable.

The peril was as nothing to the ease . . .
We five had been through death into release . . .
We stretched . . . we fell asleep . . . even I slept.

I slept not long: I shook them: 'Listen,' I said.
'I used to know Troy well before the war.
I came to spy here early in the war,
And found odd changes in the gates and roads.
They must have made many more changes since.
I must make certain what the changes are,
Before we venture more: our lives depend on't.

I am going out: I charge and order you
To stay here, still as death, till I return.
I may be gone an hour, but not more.

If I am seen and set upon, I'll shout,
If I shout *Help*, hurry to rescue me.
If I shout *Greeks*, know that you must escape.
Unhook the Horse's traces instantly,
And let yourselves over the city wall.

The parapet is not ten yards away . . .
There, past the altar.
                    When you reach the ground
Look for our comrades coming to attack.
Two of you keep awake and still as death.
And all of you wait here.
If you are found and questioned, answer this,
That you are Idan allies of King Priam
Who missed the signal when your comrades marched.
But you will not be found, if you keep still,
So wait for me. This is the safest place
In all Troy city. Do not stir from here.'

All four declared that they would do as bidden,
So out I glid into the temple yard,
In Troy, by the great stars, two hours to cock-crow.

My first excursion was to see the gate
That Agamemnon ordered us to open.
As I expected, it had been walled-up.
The very road to it impassable.
We could not open, nor our comrades enter.
So much for Agamemnon's Kingly plan.

I tried the postern gate; that, too, was walled.
No man had used it since the war began,
As I had feared: the only gate in use
Was the King's gate by which the Horse had entered.

Now that gate was beneath King Priam's palace,
Where lights still burned and guards would surely be,
How many guards? How many more, near by?

I had to try to find, finding my way.
Troy was all changed from all that I remembered,
Allies had lived in Troy, stores had been hived,
Roads blocked with huts for barracks and for barns,
And I, in moonless midnight, thief and spy,
Had to discover passage through the maze.

It took a time: much longer than I thought,
But luckily the city-dogs were gone,
(King Priam's boar-hounds), luckily for me.

And then, at last, I saw the gate-house guard.
Two men, under a lamp, playing at draughts.
Others (perhaps a dozen) stretched asleep,
And nets across the door against surprise.

I could not see how we could clear the nets,
And overcome the dozen by surprise.
Again I cursed the folly of the King
Planning such schemes, then giving me command
To do them, possible to do or not.

I crept away into a dark recess
And puzzled how we might surprise the guard.
They were too many . . . yet, perhaps, Epeios
Might scream some distance off . . . the guards might run
To quell the tumult, while we other four
Attacked those left and opened the great gate.

We should be one to three: and then the gate . . .
Barred, I could see; probably chained and locked.

Even if we killed the guard, one against three,
How open up before half Troy was roused?

I saw no way of doing the King's will.
'Possibly one among us may suggest
Some mad device that may be destiny's,'
I muttered as I turned to tell my fellows.

But as I groped the dark, a thought occurred.
'King Agamemnon seldom tells the truth,
Never the whole truth; is he fooling us?

No . . . he has something planned: some treachery,
Breaking of oath, bringing the hope of plunder.
We are a portion of the plan; but what?
Something is on its way to ruin Troy.

Are we to cause diversion, when it comes?
But can it come? or, coming, can it enter?
How can it enter, save by the King's Gate?
Here is some devilry of Agamemnon's . . .
And Menelaus must know what it is . . .
                Or are the five of us sent to be killed?
That Agamemnon may be rid of us,
And have our fiefs and ships?

Still, if the Greeks were coming to attack
They must be seen, or heard.
                                Over the rampart
I stared into the night across the plain.

I heard the hurry of wind and whimper of water.
I saw a blackness, and, far-off, a gleam
Where embers of the burnt Greek camp flared up.

There was no sight nor sound of armed men coming
Near Troy, as Agamemnon said they would.

Had they set forth, perhaps, and lost their way?
Men almost must when Agamemnons lead,
Or had they mutinied and sailed for home?

I had stayed too long: I turned to tell the four.

And, turning, I saw flickering light ahead;
Light, near the Horse . . .
                              An ember from the pan
Smashed by Kassandra had set fire to something.

That would rouse Troy . . . too true . . . a hut was burning;
Some bit of lower board . . . but what was worse.
Inside the temple of the four a voice . . .
The four were talking: yes, and had a light.
Talking, with light, in Troy . . . had they gone mad?

Were they the Four, or the killers of the Four?
The light, and voice, were both where the Four lay.

Was it a temple-priest, intoning prayer?

At least, there was no alarm, no cry, no fight.

Through the empty temple, I crept terrified.

I peered into the shrine; my heart stopped beating.

A shrouded woman's corpse holding a lamp;
A white ecstatic face was muttering bliss.

It was Kassandra talking to the God.

The Four had gone. I heard Kassandra say,
'Is it Thy doom, that Greek dogs kill the stag?
The hounds that murder stags are only dogs.
Doing allotted doom, they are but dogs;
What follows dogs that do allotted doom.'

A spirit voice said 'Doom, on tireless feet.'

The very God said that; no human throat.
A voice that clave like fire to the soul.
The light went out, the face was no more there.

I tottered out, for doom on tireless feet
Was all too near . . . had it destroyed the Four?

Where were the four? Not murdered in the temple;
Not in the Horse again, as I could see
By the flame near it; neither had they taken
The traces to escape over the rampart . . .
But they were gone, despite all oath and order.
         And now a cock crowed for an hour from dawn.
At any moment now, I might be seen.
I moved to a dark den out of the fire-light.

The four must still be near, expecting me.

As for King Agamemnon's sacking force,
It had not come, nor, if it came, could enter.

But where had the four vanished . . . yes . . . and why?

Troy was all dead asleep about me still;
Dark, often, for the fire on the hut
Lapsed down, and almost out, as the wind fell
Between the midnight gusts.
     I watched and listened.

And then a strange noise from beneath my feet,
Down in the earth, in cellar or in crypt,
Of something moving there, came to my ears,
But what could move, and make a noise like that?
A long thing, slowly moving stealthily . . . ?

Friends, Troy was holy then for a great shrine,
My Goddess' temple, near to where I hid.

I knew, too well, what horror glided there.

Long centuries since, the earliest City Troy
Stood northward, on the sacred Tamarisk Hill.
The King moved city and temples to the Hill
Where now I stood, but was afraid to move
The image of the Goddess whom I serve.

The Goddess by an earthquake clove a way
Under the ground and walked that rocky crypt
To Her new home, and there dwelt close to me.

And (as the story said) terrible snakes
Dripping cold poison, kept that secrecy
Death to all shrine-breakers and foes of Troy.

That noise beneath me was the eternal snakes
Crawling upon their scaly milkless breasts.

There in the narrow passage of the rock,
Beneath my feet, after a thousand years,
Those sightless, bloodless deaths crawled in the dark.
Crawled, now, for me, sworn servant of the goddess,
My Goddess, who had kept and counselled me . . .
I, now, her shrine-breaker and foe to Troy.

She who had ever helped . . . believe me, friends,
I needed help, then; I was terrified.
I turned towards Her door . . .

A pale streak came on the black mountain-tops.

Suddenly, women screamed inside Her temple,
The cocks of Troy crowed with a shattering cry,
The temple doors flung open, the bronze bolts snapped,
The multitudinous bright-eyed little owls
Tu-whood about the glittering Goddess' Self . . .
Two votaresses drew white fire about Her,
She spoke hot words of fire into my heart:
'Hence, hence, my servitor, as smoke on wind.
Death desecrates My House and I leave Troy.'

Leaning into the wind She sped away
The owls with fiery eyes in clouds about Her.
The olive trees beside the temple door
Shrivelled in sudden fire and fell in embers,
Lighting the bodies of Her votaresses
Dead of their wounds in casting open the doors.

In the dark temple Menelaus was shouting
Silence, to cursing soldiers stumbling there.

Then instantly I knew the terrible truth.

One of our Argive prisoners from Troy
Must by some Destiny have learned the entrance,
The earth-quake-riven entrance to the Shrine.
He, profane dog, had told the all-daring King
Wide-ruling, wider-greedy Agamemnon,
And he had dared this crime . . .
Doubtless the snakes were endless centuries dead
And now doom came, the doom that never dies,
And doom for me . . . in twenty heart-beats more.

Suddenly Menelaus came with Ajax
(Bull-head, we called him) to the temple-door
Within a knife-thrust of me as I crouched.

He said, 'You'll find him in Apollo's temple,
Beyond that burning hut . . .
You know my Brother's orders, what to do?'
'I know,' the Bull-Head answered, 'Have no fear,
Then, shall we now set on? Will you command?'

He had a famous yell, King Menelaus,
His one unusual gift: he uttered it.
And all the Greeks swarmed from the Mystery,
Yelling Troy's sudden end in fire and blood.

In fire, first, for even as they rushed
A great gust swept us with a roar of fire.

That burning hut was one of countless such,
Dry wooden stores or barracks all now blazing
With great bright flags and streamers of quick flame,
Towering round and licking up the Horse
And streaming over Troy, heaped by the wind
Fed by a thousand jars of olive oil.

The fire and surprise broke Priam's City.

The flames were blown down like a cataract
With foam of flaming rags, tatters and sparks
In the black smoke, like pestilence on wings,
And, high above, in the pearl of morning sky,
The multitudes of mountain birds were flying
South towards Egypt, crying I know not what,
Crying like curlews being the living souls
Of all old Troy, lamenting the town dead,
Doom having come there upon tireless feet.

EPILOGUE

'What did I do?' you ask me.
       'You remember.
The Goddess cried 'Hence, hence, as smoke on wind.'
The smoke blinding the plain reminded me.

You ask, 'Had they great plunder?' No, my friends.
The city was a red-hot glowing wreck
Undiggable, and unendurable.
The gold still lies among the dead men's bones
And the women and the little children murdered.
The army forced the King to sail for home.

Strange . . . but for mad Kassandra's pan of fire
Smashed on the Horse, Troy might not have been burnt.
And Agamemnon might have had the gold
Instead . . . of what he had. But . . . of myself?

My friends, the grey-eyed Goddess is my Fortune.
For Agamemnon and the other Kings
Their Destinies were as Apollo said.
Doom followed on them all on tireless feet.

KING EDWARD THE SECOND
TELLS HIS STORY

(Supposing the letter from Manuel Fieschi to King Edward the Third, to be true.)

The letter may be read in Bishop Stubbs's 'Historical Introductions to the Rolls Series', as reprinted from the Publications de la Société Archéologique de Montpellier, December 1877.

The usual story is that this King was savagely murdered in Berkeley Castle, and later buried in Gloucester Cathedral. Fieschi writes that he escaped from Berkeley just in time, stayed in hiding, at Corfe, for some months, then (on some alarm) crossed France into Italy, where he lived as a religious recluse till his death.

If this be true, the body in the tomb at Gloucester may be that of his gaoler.

So, my Son seeks to know how I escaped
From Berkeley, and am not the murdered thing
Whose embalmed ruins, mangled and mis-shaped,
Went in such glory to its burying;
About whose tomb the Benedictines sing
By day and night, and pilgrims offer gold . . .
Words cannot tell the treasures that they bring . . .
For one anointed, whom they slew of old . . .
Or think they did (the dogs) the story shall be told.

I had resigned my Crown: my Queen preferred
Mortimer to me; both wanted me dead.

My Son, the chosen King, Edward the Third,
Seemed (and has proved himself), a better head.
Men tried to kill me first by rotten bread,
By want of sleep, by chainings in the pit
Chin-deep in garbage where the blow-flies fed.
'A natural death,' they felt, 'would be more fit . . .
Murder him, yes, but leave his corpse unmarked by it.'

Still, though I suffered, I was little hurt.
Then Keepers changed, and treatment became kind.
I was allowed to sleep, and cleansed from dirt.
They said, still gentler treatment was designed.
Knowing my foreign Queen, I was not blind,
I knew I only lived from day to day.
Nearness to death was ever in my mind.
While I was living, I was in her way;
Even if she were dead, her paramour would slay.

Yet, for the nonce, I was not chained nor barred
But marked, in white clothes, as a prisoner still,
And so allowed into the castle-yard
And on the leads, and ate and drank my fill.
But as for going free . . . an iron grille
Unseen, was present, and a watch was kept,
Kept, too, by gaolers with command to kill
If once permitted bounds were over-stept.
An eye was ever on me, eye that never slept.

In hazy heat the blue September shone,
The apples shewed in colour through the leaves;
The swallows gathered and the swifts had gone
And tendrils withered at the castle-eaves.

The salt had come, for salting of the beeves;
And, lo, a rider there, out of the West.
Mortimer's Captain from the border-thieves.
I knew the dog, ambitious and unblest.
I thought 'The hour strikes; they put all to the test:'

A sudden pang of terror thrilled me through;
And yet . . . had terror now sufficient cause?
There had been shocking danger, as I knew,
But through the summer danger had had pause.
Why should the autumn bring the tiger's claws?
Into the yard, men trundled casks of beer,
They spiled and spigotted amid applause;
A steward called 'Come, gather for good cheer.
Our Harvest Ale; rejoice, for this good time of year.'

That did not sound like murder: and the crowd
Careering, cheering, passing round the can,
Was all delight and life; alive and loud.
Sin has been like a snake since it began.
Snake-like the rider was, Mortimer's man.
Murder had branded him for men to see.
But sunset was my daily freedom's span.
My jailers (all good fellows) came for me.
They led me to my room, then left, and turned the key.

Lately, my room was lit when I returned.
Tonight, it was just dim with the last glow.
No candle there, nor any fire, burned.
I stood alone and felt the darkness grow.

What if that very night I had to go
Alone, into whatever Death might bring?
Death terrifies when it comes sudden so.
Such leaving living is a dreadful thing . . .
Then, from my curtained bed a quiet voice said 'King . . .'

Before I fell, or swooned, or cried,
A man was kneeling at my side.
'King,' he hissed, 'King. I've come to save 'ee
Back to the life th' Almighty gave 'ee.
The one who sends to save 'ee so
Says 'Say, "Saint Margaret", and he'll know.'

All this, in a fierce whispered gasp.
He thrust a knife into my grasp.

The words, 'Saint Margaret', truly gave
The certainty he came to save.

'So, Friend,' I said, 'I thought aright.
They mean to murder me tonight?'

'Yes; but St Margaret has good spies . . .
First, King, put on this gray disguise.'

I did. He said 'Tonight's the time
The three are here to do the crime.
But midnight doings such as these
Must have no mortal witnesses.
To prove I'm telling true, the sounds
That rise below next, will be hounds.'

And at his words with laughing thrill
A huntsman's horn below blew shrill,
A hunter cheered, the hounds gave tongue
Like minster bell-peals being rung.

Someone was loosing kennel doors.
I' the Court, rejoicings rose in roars,
The singers at the Harvest-Ale,
Might have aroused all Severn Vale.
What with the hounds, the songs, the cheering
All devilry of Hell seemed nearing.

'You hear?' the man said. 'Listen, why,
They want no persons to be by
When they begin on what they plan.
They'll have each woman, child and man
Out of this castle in ten minutes.
They'll all be outaway like linnets,
A-hunting for a midnight stag.

This afternoon they laid a drag
(Red herring 'twas, away up top).
They've laid a bonfire for the stop;
And any one who gets so far
Can get blind drunk till Morning Star,
They've cakes and ale enough to sink
All dwellers here with food and drink.
There'll be none here, to hear or see.

Step to the wall, King, to the slit . . .
I think they've got the bonfire lit.'

They had: the wold-top had a glow.

'Now, King,' he said, 'Hark here to me . . .
You are a fighting-man, I know,
You played a pretty sword as Prince?

Myself:
   Yes, but have lost all practice since.

The Man:
   'True, but we have surprise tonight.
Surprise is more than half a fight.
And their command is 'Kill him clean;
Let never blood or wound be seen.'
They'll have no knives: ourselves have two.'

Below, the trumpet and halloo
And tumult of the hunters grew
Drink had so flown that all men yelled,
The hounds, made frantic, were still held,
While drunken men with hoick and hark
Made every dog in hearing bark.
A sergeant of the castle guard
Shouted 'Get ready, all; hold hard . . .
Three cheers, boys; one, two, three . . . Away.'
Then with a roar the whole array,
Riders, men, women, children, all
Rushed after hounds with cheer and bawl,
The hounds in cry, the huntsman horning,
All folk in yell like Judgment Morning.
The tumult lessened up the hill.

III

The fortress of my jail was still
Save for one drunkard whom I heard
Mocking the June-glad turtle-bird;
Sometimes he cock-a-doodle-dood.

The castle was a solitude,
The hunting uproar failed and died.

There was a stealthy step outside,
Someone came dragging something there
Onto the landing from the stair,
Thence to a little room next mine.
What part was this in the design?
What did he drag, that seemed like stuff,
But yet had scarcely room enough?

The dragger dumped the thing, and turned,
And suddenly a lantern burned:
Someone had thrust it on the floor
Outside, within the corridor.

Then, as the sounds made us aware,
Two men came cursing what they bare,
Something with fiery crumbs that fell
That made them curse by Death and Hell,
A brazier, as I judged, alight.
They were two creatures of the night,
Footsteps and curses were all muffled.

Words muttered and the footsteps shuffled
In the next room, preparing crime.

The doing took a little time
Then they went down; then, a door closed
(The sergeants' mess-door, I supposed).
The castle seemed devoid of men.

The drunkard hooted now and then.

'King,' the man said, 'The time is near.
The man will bring your supper here.
Bread manchets, and an earthen jug
Of pottage mixed with sleepy drug,
To stun you with; the man's the boor
They call Black Lousy or the Moor.
I think he'll come alone tonight . . .

If so, he must not bark nor bite.

He'll put your supper on the floor,
And fumble to unlock the door . . .
The instant the door opens, King,
Heave it wide open, with a swing,
Before he knows whose pig has died
I'll have him, with his keys, inside,
With a bat upon his head or so.

But life is troublous here below.
The dog may come with all the three,
Still, swing the door and take the key,
I'll see the Moor laid quiet; then
We two will knife the other men.

Remember, King, they'll have no knives,
They dare not knife you for their lives.
'No bloodshed,' say these dogs of sin,
'But burn his insides out within':
That's why they've brought the brazier there.'

Again the terror in me stirred;
Who was this fellow who had heard
All the whole plot to murder me?
A man whose face I could not see . . .
A sudden secret man unknown,
And vouched for by two words alone.
Could he be Murderer the First,
The falsest, deadliest and worst?

He said, 'My King, all will be well.
St Margaret against all Hell.
St Margaret knows what they intend
And she's a friend, and I'm a friend,
We'll get you out tonight I trust,
We've starlight in us besides dust.
You swing the door back, King, and trust.'

'I do,' I said, I shook his hand.
'But, friend, my murder has been planned
By men who will pursue until
At last they run me down and kill . . .
What if I do escape from here?'

'A Saint'll help from far and near'
He answered, 'Now, get ready, sure,
Behind the door, here comes the Moor.'

Below upon the stair, the singer
Was certainly my supper-bringer.
He sang or gurgled lines and snatches
Of drinking-songs and three-man catches.
He was alone – or was he? Yes . . .
I took my place in readiness.
My comrade gripped his bludgeon handle
The Moor set down his tray and candle
Outside my door
                        'These Kings,' said he.
He had some trouble with the key
(The wards caught in his belt, I think.)
'Hey piggy, swill-time, come and drink.'
He called 'You Edward, come, sup sorrow.
You'll have few body-slaves tomorrow.'

Then, kicking at the door, he bawled,
'Come out, you Edward, when you're called.'
While fitting-in the key he cursed:
Then kicked, and shoved, and in he burst.
The bludgeon stretched him on the floor.
We dragged his body from the door,
Then locked him in and took the key.

We listened for where foes might be.

The bats about the battlement
Were shrilling as they came and went.

Some horses were below, at food,
Stamping and munching as they stood.

I wondered whose the horses were
I had not heard them enter there.

Near them, the drunken man still sat
Mewing, at odd times, like a cat.

No other noise of living men
Stirred in the vast grim prison pen.

Then, as we listened there, we heard
Below, not near, that some-one stirred.
A door was opened, a voice cried
'Is that you, Lousy?' none replied.

After some seconds, the door closed.

The coast was clear as we supposed.
Now by the light in that grim place
I first beheld my comrade's face,
A good face for a troublous time.

What had they readied for the crime,
In that next room three paces thence?
A pan of fire, smoking dense,
Some rags and ropes and thoughts of hell.
'Come, King' my comrade said, 'All's well . . .'
He led the way to a stair's shaft
Up which the cool night blew a draft.

Downstairs, he led, making no sound.
In a dark dimness, round on round,
Feeling for steps we could not see,
Each step a freedom won for me.

Sudden, his reached hand halted me.

The drunken man had changed his note,
He bleated like a nanny goat.
The munching of the nags was clear
I heard no sound of danger near.
My friend leaned back and whispered close . . .
'A sentry's there . . . his shadow shows . . .
The wall there . . . when the rushlight blows . . .'

I craned: I peered: the wall below,
Rush-lighted, had a shadow show
The helmed head of a man-at-arms,
Ready to smite or raise alarms.

I whispered 'Friend . . . it's neck or knives.'

The thing men dread seldom arrives:
Just as we tiptoed down to dare
The terror vanished into air.
The helmed head was a shadow thrown
From a carved column on the stone.

We passed . . . we felt the cool damp grace
Of autumn mist on hand and face,
The horses lifted heads, and blew . . .
We passed: and then 'One moment . . . you'.
A sleeper by the horses roused . . .
He caught me by the sleeve, half-drowsed.

'Is the work finished yet, upstairs?'
Friends, I was taken unawares,
But something checked me; not to kill,
This was some stable-boy who knew
Nothing of what men meant to do . . .
'Why, no,' I said, 'Nor will be yet . . .
Son, lie you down, sleep and forget . . .
They'll call you . . . you're to carry word?'
I'll guess you're the Queen's pigeon-bird?'

'Yes,' the lad said, 'Our lovely Queen . . .'

'The loveliest lady ever seen,'
I said, 'God send her lovelier men . . .
Now sleep.' The boy lay down agen.

We were in mist: we were in dew:
We heard the midnight owls tu-whoo,
We trod the yard, we passed the gate.
Some cottagers were still up late
Eyeing the ruddy distant glare,
The bonfire where the hunters were.
'Good night,' they said, 'Good night,' said I.

There was the Pole Star in the sky,
This England's Hope Star never dead . . .
We kept the track as the star led.

Soon, in a copse, was my Saint Margaret friend
With horses, money, letters, and a scheme
To bring my present dangers to an end:
She brought a dawning to my night's extreme.

I was afar when morning 'gan to gleam;
I was in safety when I stopped to rest;
Kingdom and Queen and peril all a dream,
Naught but confusion without interest,
My past sponged from the slate, my future manifest.

A year from thence, again she rescued me
(My enemies suspected where I hid);
Hearing the plot she plucked me over sea
Her spirit wrought whatever minds forbid.
I traversed France my direst foes amid.
Here on her bounty now I live in peace,
Hermit, in Italy, forever rid
Of earth's rebellions, I enjoy release
And find that lacking much assures the soul's increase.

KING EDWARD'S PRAYER

O King of all things Who appointed me
To rule a Kingdom from an earthly throne,
And saw me humbled from that dignity
Because of fault in measure seldom known,
O King, Who helped when I was all alone,
Setting a light in one remembering heart
That fused the lock and smote aside the stone
So that I dwell forgotten and apart,
Nothing as living man but conscious what Thou art,

I do beseech Thee to remember Her
Who in my peril, saved me out of ward;

Let elemental angels minister
As her defences ever, helm and sword.
Gladden her grasses, let her barns be stored
With cattle, poultry, grain, corn, honey, wine,
Whatever sun and earth and rain afford,
Whatever wealth I gladdened-in, when mine,
And may her soul help men to make this Kingdom Thine.

Here, in the twilight, in a foreign cell,
I pray for her, that Margaret the Blest,
Who snatched me from the pangs of plotted Hell,
And still lives Severn-wards, or further West,
A relic still of all I loved the best,
That woman in the darkness scarcely seen
There at the cross-roads under Birdlip Crest,
She who preserved me from what would have been,
O may her skies be blue, her sunny pathways green.

A CRY TO MUSIC

Speak to us, Music, for the discord jars;
The world's unwisdom brings or threatens Death.
Speak, and redeem this misery of breath
With that which keeps the stars
Each to her point in the eternal wheel
That all clear skies reveal.

Speak to us; lift the nightmare from us; sing.
The screams of chaos make the daylight mad.
Where are the dew-drenched mornings that we had
When the lithe lark took wing?
Where the still summers, when more golden time
Spoke to us, from the lime?

Though these be gone, yet, still, Thy various voice
May help assuage the pangs of our distress,
May hush the yelling where the fiends rejoice,
Quiet the sleepless, making sorrow less.
Speak, therefore, Music; speak.
Calm our despair; bring courage to the weak.

Ah, lovely Friend, bring wisdom to the strong,
Before a senseless strength has all destroyed.
Be sunlight on the night of brooding wrong.
Be form upon the chaos of the void.
Be Music; be Thyself; a prompting given
Of Peace, of Beauty waiting, and sin shriven.

THE PRINCESS MALINAL

'Destiny's Sword,' this Cortés, whom you praise?
He was 'Malinche', in his earlier days
Ere conquest was, or chance of it began.
What does 'Malinche' mean? 'Malinal's Man'.
My Man, for I am Malinal, my friends,
One used by Destiny for marvellous ends.
I, Malinal, through whom it came to pass
That Mexico was mown like the ripe grass.

What was that Mexico? No old estate,
Wise with long centuries of splendid Fate,
No, but a land whose heart-blood soaked the sods
In daily sacrifice to loathsome gods,
Brought to us by the Aztec conqueror
In lust and terror three men's lives before,
Who were the Aztecs? No man living knows.
Grim warriors from the desert, bearing bows.

I am the Daughter of a Prince whose realm
The Aztecs taxed, but did not overwhelm.

There, in my youth, the Prince, my Father, died.
Another Kinglet of that countryside
Married my Mother, and they had a Son.

My childhood thence was an unhappy one.
I was a pest of which they would be rid
But shrank from killing;
                              this is what they did.
They gave me as a pupil to a band
Of minstrel-dancers roving through the land
Singing and miming many an ancient lay.
And, as a slave-girl died that very day,
They said that Princess Malinal had died,
And buried her, as me, in princely pride,
While I, the Princess, went as Fortune willed.

But, yet, those Indians of the dancing guild
As Indians of our old religion, knew
That gods allot a rank as Justice due,
To them, I was Princess, born to great things,
They tended me in all our wanderings,
They taught me all the dancing and the mime
That helped all songs of the heroic time
And wandering always up and down the land
I learned the tongues and came to understand
What hot intensity of hate and dread
King Montezuma and his priesthood bred.
For all her beauty Mexico was hell,
The tribes about her panted to rebel.

Among our singings to the passers-by,
There was a poem of a prophecy,
That when the appointed centuries had run
Then, from the sea, the Children of the Sun,
A pale-faced people coming in strange ships,

Would put our ancient glories in eclipse
And govern Mexico from sea to sea . . .
Our hearers prayed that this might swiftly be,
And signs were present that the time was near,

A pale-faced set of seamen had put fear,
Some years before, along our eastern coast,
One of those seamen, looking like a ghost
Was shown to me, slave to an eastern chief.
'I came for gold,' he said, 'But have found grief.'

My childhood passed; and soon, with gun and horse,
The pale-face from the sunrise came in force,
No Children of the Sun, but landless braves,
Seeking for gold and concubines and slaves;
Devils they seemed, with slaughter in command,
Bent both to plunder and possess the land.
The country chieftains rallied and attacked,
The Spaniards stood: the coastal towns were sacked,
And in the war, that Spaniard was set free
Who, like a corpse's ghost, had talked to me.
He spoke our tongue, and was a prize untold,
Worth more to Cortés then than any gold.
Now, after battle murderous to both,
He could speak peace: the Indians were not loath.

There after battle, through this rescued slave,
A treaty sprang; one promised, one forgave.
The Indians (who forgave) promised to send
Gifts as a splendid pledge that wars should end.

I, Malinal, began then, as I deem,
Life became action that had been a dream.

Suddenly, Chieftains let their subjects know
That twenty of their prettiest girls should go
Among the many gifts of gold and food,
Raiment and cloth, to make the treaty good.
A hundred girls cast lots, one from each five,
To mix with gods whom we thought death to wive,
There I, by Fate appointed, stood aghast. . .
I, a Princess, one of the twenty cast.

Rail not at Fate and strive to be forgiving,
Justice is ever done on all things living.
I, Malinal, a Princess born, perceived
These things were men, not gods as we believed,
Men of an unknown type, exceeding strange,
But men of power, able to bring change,
Eager to change, and my young spirit knew
My woman's wit could guide them what to do.
I saw, at once, that these might rip to wreck
The Aztec chains about the subject neck,
Destroy the accursed priests upon the stairs
Red with the hearts torn to those gods of theirs;
And free from tyranny and tax and dread
All native tribes as yet not stricken dead;
This I perceived; and, then . . . that slave set free . . .
Who knew our tongues could teach and answer me.

I am a Princess born; no thing of shame,
I was their Queen in everything but name,

A Queen quick-witted, too, swiftly aware
Of rivals plotting against Cortés there.
Spaniards in Cuba, grim ambitious men
Arming to fight his army, even then.
Meaning to seize his conquests and be great
By his adventurings, those dogs of hate.

There, in the West, in Mexico, our King,
Great Montezuma watched what time would bring,
Hoping that, where we lay, his eastern chiefs
Would slaughter all these pirates of his fiefs.
Presuming on these hopes, he would do naught
But send fair words . . .
                                    such was this woman's thought.

And thinking thus, I saw the chances given.
Slow is man's pace; swift is the light of Heaven.
Northward and westward still some tribes remained
Doomed by the Aztecs but not yet enchained;
These, I perceived, would come at Cortés' call,
With these as allies Mexico might fall.

Clear in each detail all the project showed.
Instant the scheme, but difficult the road,
Yet daily, Cortés found my instinct true,
We made strong friends, advanced and overthrew,
We crossed the snowy stones in the bleak blast,
We reached the marvel of the world at last;
We, scarce four hundred men, achieved the way,
The darkness brightened: there the City lay.

Could it exist, or did it only seem,
That shining thing, that city of a dream?
We, who had come from deserts and from snows,
Saw a blue lake, from which the temples rose;
Blue as the Heaven the lake, the city bright
With burnished lime too glitteringly white . . .
The lake dotted with barges, crossed by ways
Thronged with such crowds it put us in amaze,
The crowds so glorious with gold and gear
That liker birds than men they did appear . . .
But then the birds were there, brighter than they,
The humming bird, flamingo, popinjay,
In trees so decked with fruit, scarlet and gold,
So fragrant with sweet gums, of worth untold,
In grass so green, with flowers so red and white
That all was the soul's marvel and delight,
All a conspiring culminating thing,
For gold, above all metal else, the King,
The gold-deckt, feather-gleaming Montezume,
Whose Paradise had this for ante-room.

Was this, the death-trap that our allies feared?
This marvel, more a marvel as we neared?
To mortal men alive beneath the Sun
Some cups are there to drink, and this was one.
And though our allies bade us, 'O beware,
Never go in, for they will kill you there.'
I trusted in my instinct what to do,
Malinal's Man, Malinche, trusted, too.

Yet, being in the city, doubts and fears
Sprang to my mind as whispers reached my ears.

We held a builded island in a lake,
Deep water round us, this was one mistake.
To reach the shore were causeways not our own,
Causeways with bridges easily o'erthrown;
Easily barred, or taken in the flank
By archers in canoes from either bank.

Malinche had no fear: I doubted . . . I.
We lived in splendour, and the days went by.

There, in the splendour I interpreted
For both the leaders and the chiefs they led,
Perceiving clearly that the lust for gold
In Cortés' captains would not be controlled,
And that the Aztecs were of one advice,
To give us to their gods in sacrifice.
There, in the splendour, I was swiftly sure
That peace, near so much gold, could not endure,
That war, near so much hatred, must be close,
Though falsehood in both chiefs contrived a gloze.

Having beheld the gold, it was not long
Before Malinche launched into the wrong,
Seized Montezuma's person and prepared
To fight for all that gold, if any dared.

Before that moment came, his Cuban foes
In greed and envy thought to interpose;
Having great friends in Spain they gathered men
From all the landless lusts in Cuba then;

Having great wealth, they armed a fleet of ships
And planning battle, murder and eclipse,
Westward they sailed, just at that touch of time
When Cortés' spirit swayed twixt peace and crime.
Straightway they landed near our harbour base,
Three times our strength to bring us to disgrace,
To seize our havings, and with hate and greeds
Snatch all the crop where we had sown the seeds;

This at the moment when our fortunes there
Within the city, swayed upon a hair.

Friends, any instant's peril raised a thirst
In Cortés' heart to meet the peril first.
Back to his base he marched; by force and guile
He quelled that peril in a little while;
By tact and bribes he won his beaten foes
To help him bring his conquests to a close.
Westward to Mexico he marched in pride,
As conquering King I saw Malinche ride.

Brightly his star had shone, but now it paled;
His foes were quelled, but now disease assailed.
A negro slave brought by the Cubans West
Died there of small-pox spreading death and pest.
As sudden windflaws fan a spark to blaze,
So did that one infection kill and craze,
Many among us died, and all who died
Spread death and dying through the countryside.

Like forest-fire, in a gale it spread,
That spotted evil, smiting thousands dead;
And ere we breathed (the Cuban danger quelled)
As one mad man all Mexico rebelled.

Rage upon rage, with Montezuma killed,
All my instinctive terrors were fulfilled.
Now in the midnight came the fearful snowing
Of stones and darts, death-horns, death-whistles blowing,
The causeways blocked, the bridges cut, the lake
Thronged with canoes to spear us or to take.
In battle, in rain falling, we were driven
(The few survivors) from our shining Heaven
Hunted like starving dogs, stoned, sleepless, hurt,
Stumbling and fighting, blind with blood and dirt.
Leaving our wounded to the priesthood's knives
On altars clotted black with Spanish lives,
Or drowning in the water weighted down
With cursed gold from that accursed town . . .
Now burning, smoking ruin heaped with dead.

Before the dawn, we halted as we fled
To bind our bleedings underneath the tree,
Malinal's Man there asked advice of me.

Friends, my advice decided Mexico.

No other of us knew to whom to go;
No other than myself knew what could save.
The counsel none but I could give I gave.
I told what Indian allies would be true.

And true they were, and so I speak to you;
And Cortés won the land from sea to sea.

Long afterwards, we travelled, I and he,
Through Mexico, to make new ways begin.
I, Malinal, again beheld my Kin,
Mother, Step-father and usurping heir,
All terror-stricken, kneeling in the glare,
I, Malinal, might judge in my own case.

I took my Mother into my embrace:
I cried, 'O welcome, Mother, to your own.
Step-father, too; let gladnesses atone.
Little half-brother, whom I hardly knew,
O welcome, all . . . let life begin anew.'

But what is Life? A something swift and strange
Fulfilling justice in eternal change;
A passage to perfection and decline
Through hopes unspeakable in waste design;
A something ever helped by things unseen
That glorifies the King and crowns the Queen,
That makes an empire rise, a Kingdom die,
By one like Cortés linked with such as I.

MEMORIES

Now that the leaves are withered, fallen, or falling,
Their greenness is a ghost beyond recalling.

Yet, of those ghosts of greenness, to a ghost,
Which awakes joy, and is remembered most?

Which, in the cuckoo-time of blue-bell May,
Promised most marvel on the kindled spray,

Seemed most alive?
              Thus, as survivors use,
I think of withered leaves and strive to choose.

Out of the hundreds of remembered dead
Of days long past, comes one illumined head,

The cloaked and sworded foreign Prince who sought
To try all feeling and to plumb all thought;

The Palace-born, from infancy made wise,
In all the graces and the courtesies,

Reminding all of Gautama, the Prince,
Who gave up home and Kingdom centuries since,

To seek, in inmost thought's intensest air,
A meaning in the ills that mortals bear,
A hope of ending of the burden borne.

Like Gautama, that Star of the forlorn,
His spirit struggled, inly consecrate
To wander Hell until he found a gate.

Like Gautama, he moved men as he stood
In the pale beauty of his hardihood.

Like Gautama, his Vision unattained,
He moved men so, the thought of him remained.

On vastly different tracks we had to tread
And life's divergence made him as one dead.

And Life imposed its multitudes and miles
And Change, and Chance, for many weary whiles.

Often all unexpected and unsought
Comes the completion of profoundest thought.

A generation made his memory dim;
I was far hence, and had no thought of him.

I watched the sunburnt men in vintage-time,
I passed them up the hill I had to climb.

I clambered stairs, upon whose balustrade
Grotesque great gourds of green and gold were laid.

And passing these, upon the topmost stair,
He called me by my name, for he was there.

Changed, as a Prince is changed, who becomes King,
Well might the grape-men of the vineyard sing.

He had attained the Light under his tree.
A sunlit day, a sunburned day to me.

MIDDLE FARM
or
THE CHERRIES

'Cherries and bread, for Man's delight, and need,
His pleasure and his very life, the two,
Fostered by sun and rain, and soil and seed,
And by the sweat of Man, the season through.
Bases of all that mortals are and do;
Sweet juice and corn, that never did men harm.'
So my thought runs at Harwell Middle Farm.

In April woods, the white wild-cherry-flowers
Toss in their glory before leaves appear.
Banners and vanguard of the jolly hours,
The blackbird hatched, cuckoo and swallow near.
And though the blossom bring but fruit austere
That only birds enjoy, this April white
Is Spring, her very self, and man's delight.

Once, far away, past Troy, the rich-in-gold,
Before the ship-wright's axe the forests felled,
Great, sweet, transparent cherries grew of old,
There, where the Amazonian hunters dwelled,
Exquisite, healing cherries, precious held,
So that when Asia fell to conquering Rome,
Captain Lucullus carried cuttings home.

Two thousand years have gone, since those two stocks
(Crossed with how many others?) have been tried
Among the bees at each Spring Equinox,
By countless testers, ever watchful-eyed.
From many a climate, many a country-side,
The variants come, too many for my tale,
Sweet, bitter, bitter-sweet, black, scarlet, pale.

Though the unknown may ever seem more fair
Than the dull known of every day's event,
Though many wonders may be, or once were,
One little island is our continent;
England's our life, of joy or discontent,
And we, who sail so far, had better turn
To English fields, the cherry-lore to learn.

There is a gray stretch of the Berkshire chalk,
Horn Down, and Harwell Field, and Hagbourne Hill
Where pale blue flowers crown the chicory stalk
In late Julys whenever corn-ears fill,
Below, where the springs burst and the brooks trill,
Long centuries since, men found that cherries throve
For Harwell Man's perpetual treasure-trove.

Thus it is still, in all this quiet scene,
In old-time fields, in farms that Doomsday knew,
The Cherry governs as the Harvest Queen
And world-wide crossings stock the fields anew.
The sun, the Earth, the bees, the rain, the dew,
These five remain, and man's inspired skill
Beguiles the five to bring the Cherry still.

Though there be aptitude in soil that feeds
Or holds especial guard that may avail,
With life and safety, certain stocks and seeds,
(And such-like cherish Cherries in the Vale),
Yet it is manly efforts that prevail
Against the odds, hard work, unceasing care,
Insight and skill, that bring the Cherries there.

For when the dead year's leaves go lingering past
In dense November drizzle, to the soil,
And tired Nature goes to rest at last,
Her last red apples hoarded-up as spoil,
Then men, just done with harvest, begin toil,
Begin again the old work everywhere
Another Summer's cherries to prepare.

They clean the fields and burn: the bonfires smoke:
They plough, manure and prune: they plant young trees:
They hack the tangles where the ditches choke:
They spray the orchards against all disease.
And March, with lengthening light, brings lesser ease . . .
Battles with Codlin-Moth, the planters' grief,
Sawfly, Red Spider, Scab and Silver-Leaf.

Then April comes, with blossom and suspense,
Lest frost should blast, or tempest sweep away,
And hourly the warfare grows more tense
As sunshine hatches-out the pests of May.
The summer comes with watching and with spray,
Laburnum-time, syringa-time, and June,
When Jack of Dover goes to bed at noon.

Then (after dog-rose time) the English rose,
High summer, and red cherry, and full joy,
The nightless summer when the cuckoo goes,
When every bird is as a little boy,
A winged imp, to threaten and annoy,
To peck the ripening cherries, and to thieve
The sweet-fleshed fruit from dewy dawn to eve.

Then, when all seems assured, the fight begins,
From before summer dawn till cats are gray,
Rattles and pebbles within shaken tins,
Clackage and scarecrows to keep birds away;
And men with shotguns all the summer day
Shot after shot; much battle, but few dead,
Wherever birds are swift or cherries red.

And as the battle bangs, the picking starts,
Into the field the sunburned pickers fare,
With ladders, baskets and collecting carts
And tree by tree is mounted and stripped bare.
And in the Barn, the marketers prepare:
The Barn whose builders ceased to work or sing
Ere Wesley preached, or George the Third was King.

All know the English Barn; the simple nave;
The transepts, with their doors; the timbered roof
So lovely with the grace the builders gave,
Yet centuries-strong (and English-weather-proof);
With darkness where the great owls keep aloof,
And jackdaws nest, cats kitten, swallows dive;
The harvest home that keeps mankind alive.

There, in the Barn, the white chip-baskets spread,
Rank upon rank with all the various kinds,
The pale, the red and gold, the black and red,
Each the bright fruit of many thinking minds.
The sunlight gives the colour of the rinds
Lustre, like jewels, till the barn-floor seems
Treasure beyond an Eastern Prince's dreams.

There now the hungry cherry-lovers come,
To taste and choose, to buy and bear away,
The motors hoot, the lorry-engines hum
Twixt gate and barn the well-known narrow way,
And through the dusty, sweet, hot summer day,
More and more baskets come-in from the field
Where sunburned men secure the season's yield.

Something of summer's beauty crowns the place;
Much of the summer bounty blesses there
All of these cherry-folk with quiet grace,
Welcome and peace, that cherry-buyers share.
Harvest brings Nature's kindness everywhere,
The sweetness of reward on Summer's crest
That men wring from the earth that gives them rest.

It is great peace to watch the quiet scene
Of Nature's bounty, won by toil and skill.
May Middle Farm's fair orchards flourish green
And happy harvests many baskets fill,
As long as chicory on Hagbourne Hill
At cherry-harvest opens blossoms blue,
And reddening cherries glisten in the dew.

IN PRAISE OF NURSES

Dedicated to
MARY CLIFFORD
LAURA FRANKLIN
HELEN MCKENNA
PHYLLIS SIMMONDS
JOANNA WILLS

Man, in his gallant power, goes in pride,
Confident, self-sufficient, gleaming-eyed,
Till, with its poison on an unseen point
A sickness strikes and all his strengths disjoint.
Then, helpless, useless, hideous, stinking, mad,
He lies bereft of what he was and had,
Incapable of effort, limb and brain,
A living fog of fantasies of pain.

And yet, today, as ever, since man was,
Even mad Man a healing impulse has.
Doctors there are, whose wisdoms know and check
The deadly things that bring the body's wreck,
Who minish agony, relieve and heal
Evils once mortal in Man's commonweal.
All honour Doctors; let me honour those
Who tend the patient when the doctor goes.

Daily and nightly, little praised or paid,
Those ordered, lovely spirits bring their aid,
Cheering the tired when the pain is grim,
Restoring power to the helpless limb.

Watching through darkness, driving away fear
When madness brings her many spectres near;
Cleansing the foul, and smiling through the pique
Of nerves unstrung or overstrained or weak,
Bringing to all a knowledge, hardly won,
Of body's peace and spirit's unison;
And blessing pillows with a touch that brings
Some little ease to all man's broken strings.

All that they do is utter sacrifice
Of all themselves and precious beyond price;
And what a joy, through them, to re-survey
That narrow, sweet, now half-forgotten way
Of selfless service as a way to live
Based not on what you win but what you give.

Daily these gentle souls give pain relief:
Deferring dying they diminish grief;
The one they succour need not be a friend,
Only a wreck with anguish to amend.
Anguishes such as lately made me see
Such day-and-night-devotion given to me.

To you, most beautiful, devoted friends,
My gratitude will go until life ends.

Never, while living, may I fail to bless
The thought of you about my wretchedness.

I thank and bless you: that I write at all
Is, by itself, your work's memorial.

THE HAWTHORNS AT THE
CHANTRY DOOR

Outside the little Chantry, built of old,
In midmost greenest May the cuckoo tolled.
Beside the doorless door where swallows swept
Two hawthorn trees a sleepless sentry kept,
One red, one white, with boughs that intertwined,

And I was ware, that each had human mind,
Life, too, intense; the red one spoke to me.

The Red Thorn
We were unhappy lovers, I and she,
She, Wife to Raimond, once this County's Lord,
Margaret, She, the honoured, the adored;
And I, the poet Guillem, laurel-wreathed,
Singer of songs, when I was man and breathed.

Let no-one think that ours was guilty love.
Though each loved other neither knew thereof.
I, like the other poets everywhere,
Praised what her noble beauty made aware,
Womanhood's glory, the one star that shows
In this blind nightmare where man's spirit goes.

The White Thorn
   Raimond, my Husband, both by mind and birth
   Felt himself God-appointed to rule earth.
   Pride was his curse, the pride of one who springs
   From all a thousand years of almost kings.

   And lesser pride, of one who ever led,
   In effort or affair the certain head.
   I knew I gathered glory, marrying him,
   But Satan as a husband can be grim.
   O terrible to bear the hourly curse
   Of pride of birth, of intellect, of purse,
   All unrelieved by one least littlest grain
   Of sense of others' hope, or joy or pain.
   I came to live in dread of his success
   Seeing it make him ever merciless.
   And yet, he had a standard, and a style.

The Red Thorn
   We have been hawthorns here a weary while.
   The while we lived, a much-loved Feast remained,
   A Court of Love at which a Lady reigned
   For whom all poets fashioned songs in praise
   And sang them to her on the singing days,
   The one whom she approved, she crowned with bays.
   Some thirty poets of the country round
   Were heard and judged, and I was the one crowned.

   My poem, as I said, praised Womanhood,
   Not Margaret's self; and this all understood.
   And Raimond knew it when his Wife crowned me.

144

But though no shadow of man's love could be
In such a song, I, making it, well knew
What hell was that bright spirit's daily due,
There with that Satan of ancestral pride
In which all beauty withered, all hope died.
So that, in writing, pity had a part;
The formal song had something from my heart.

The White Thorn
  What human heart gives life to cannot die.
  None saw that something: no-one, only I . . .
  It came as dew of healing and relief . . .
  O, it was snowdrop in my winter grief,
  It made my misery a little thing.

  Mark, now, the end:
                      Persaunt, the Eastern King,
  Came, seeking wisdom, through the western realms,
  And finding, haply, fewer brains than helms.
  This Persaunt, in his progress, was now near
  The river-frontier seven miles from here.
  Our King resolved to bid him to a feast.
  All wondered much which soldier, noble, priest,
  Provost or legist should be honoured thus
  As herald from our great King glorious,
  To bid this marvellous Indian be his guest.
  My Raimond said, 'My house is ancientest.
  My birth the noblest, and my blood more blue
  Than any King's: the office is my due.
  I shall be sent: no other has a chance.

By brain, by lineage, by inheritance,
I am the only noble qualified.'

He named what Knights of his estate should ride,
In company with him: he decked them fair
All blue and white, with bannerols to bear.
New housings for the horses, gilded spurs,
And scarlet daglets to the minivers . . .
All this assuming that the right was his.
He had no shadow of a doubt of this.

Then publicly, the King's will was proclaimed.
Guillem, not Raimond, was the envoy named.
Guillem, not Raimond, picked . . . and even worse
Guillem, not Raimond, was to write the verse
For choristers to sing in the guest's praise.

There our lives' efforts ended in a blaze.
Raimond collapsed into the pit of hell . . .
Nay, Raimond died; a fiend within him fell.

Consider . . . there were fifty people by,
When Gareth told of Guillem's embassy.
We were at dinner . . . Raimond screamed, and leant
And bit his goblet till the silver bent,
Then, rising, ordered Gareth to be still . . .
Then, glaring round for somebody to kill
Gurgled and clutched his throat and turned to me . . .
'Guillem,' he said, 'the bard who honoured thee . . .
Yes, you adulterous hag, your paramour,
Guillem, your spotted cuckoo-bard, the pure.
The King loves him, like you.'

        He struck me then
I'th' face, with's goblet, before all the men.
Then beat them from the presence, leaving me.

The Red Thorn
    Almost the instant that he let her be . . .
    I, Guillem, entered to her weeping there,
    White, with blood trickling through disordered hair . . .
    Outraged and mute, a marble of Despair.
    I saw that she was stricken to the soul . . .
    But how to shew I knew, and how console?
    Who can endure to have his sorrow known?
    In utter sorrow mortals stand alone.
    Yet I was bearer of such thrilling news,
    That utter them I must: I could not choose.
    'Lady,' I said, 'I galloped here to say,
    King Persaunt of the East is on his way
    To visit Raimond and yourself today.
    Knowing you both the Kingdom's noblest born,
    He brings the Order of the Unicorn,
    The greatest honour of his Eastern land . . .
    Given to none save by the monarch's hand.
    I could not choose but gallop to declare
    The happy honour, that you might prepare.'

    But what are happy tidings to Despair?
    I know not if she heard or understood,
    That white death silent save for drip of blood.
    So, staring and aghast, with mumbled word
    (Comfort-politeness) that she never heard,
    I stumbled thence, for Raimond must be told.

I knew the castle household from of old . . .
I met one of his men, who recommended
I leave the Count until his mood were ended.
I said, 'I could not, for the matter pressed.'
He said, 'Nay, Master, leave it, you were best:
The Count is no fit company today.'
'I bring him golden news that cannot stay.'
'Nay, Master, any news may make him worse.
Sin runs his course and Satan runs his curse . . .
He's in the garden-close; but, Master, leave . . .
An hour of wait may save a year of grieve.'
I said, 'King Persaunt's coming cannot wait.'
So, having said, I passed the garden gate.

This was at midmost May-time much as now
All scent in air, all blossom upon bough.
And there was Raimond, snarling-mad, apart
Stabbing a book of poems to the heart,
Sneering, with clenched teeth shewing in a grin,
And all hell-fire scorching him within.

He rose to's feet in silence seeing me.
'Guillem,' he said, 'the man I longed to see.
Guillem, who called my Countess Queen of Spring.
Guillem, who made me cuckold, as men sing.
Guillem, the herald to the Indian King,
Guillem, the chosen for the sacred song . . .
Or so his silly head thinks; thinking wrong.
Wrong, do you see? Wrong as this iron shows.'

I felt his cold knife in repeated blows.
I saw his dog's teeth dimming, and grass growing.
And hate, and beauty, blurring out of knowing.
And then a nothing clear, but something red
Playing like flames of hell about my head . . .
Then, something like a bird's song, as it seemed,
Now up, now down, as in a music dreamed.'

The White Thorn
   Most fatal was that day to all of us.
   Ere the day ended, I was ended, thus.
   In that same sunlight, at a later hour
   I walked the leads upon the castle tower . . .
   There Raimond came, with servants bringing wine.
   They laid it down, and left us at a sign:
   Red wine it was, with honey, and a glass.
   And Raimond, seeming penitent, alas,
   As many times before, that one-time lover.
   A useless shewing, for our lives were over.

   'Now Margaret,' he said (he seemed to smile)
   'Fury will make men mad a little while,
   Then passes . . . and repentance is begun.
   With grief for foul things said and vile things done.
   Such I have done, and would undo, unsay.
   May we forget our moment's hell today?
   May we, in friendship, drink a loving cup?'
   I bowed, he poured the glass and held it up
   Then, with his dagger, dipping honey, stirred.
   And gave to me, deep-bowing, with this word:

'Drink, lovely Margaret, the cup of peace.
Forgive my madness; let this hatred cease.'

I knew him for most evil when most suave,
But, being woman, took the cup he gave,
And drank, and thanked, and said, 'And will you drink?'
He smiled his toothy smile, 'Not so, I think.
This stirrer of your dram, this little knife,
One hour ago drank deep your lover's life,
Your Guillem's heart; below, in the green plot.
It has unloosed your pretty lover's knot,
That was so sweet; this little knife and I.
His was the life your drink was sweetened by . . .
You found it pleasant, eh? you, hag of hell?

There, in the bluebells and dead asphodel
You'll find his body stretched, so marked by me
You may not recognise him when you see.
Say . . . was it sweet, the loving-cup you drank?'
Then I:
        'So sweet, that, I shall ever thank
        All spirits of all love, that I have known
        My Guillem's spirit to the inmost bone.'
We were upon the castle-leads alone.

'And now,' I said, 'though Guillem never knew
That I adored him, be it known to you.
And know moreover how my soul is thrilled
That I am dying, Guillem being killed,
And pass in ecstasy to my eclipse,
His life like sacrament upon my lips.'

So, being at the battlements, I leaped
And only knew of something senseless heaped
Where there were stones and little toad-flax flowers.

King Persaunt laid us in this tomb of ours,
Guillem and me, and built the chapel here,
Beautiful once, but ruined many a year;
While, as for Raimond, he was prisoned close,
For many years enduring many woes,
But linked to us, still, by the lasting chain.

The Red Thorn
But, Margaret: see: rejoice: he comes again.
The time for setting free has run its sands.
In happier forms and days in wiser lands
We shall again endeavour, and be wise,
And all the joy-bells ring in Paradise.
Look, here is Raimond . . . how the joy-bells ring.'

I heard the thrushes and the blackbirds sing
For the exceeding beauty of the Spring,
And tiny hawthorn blossoms white and red
Fell light as sins forgiven on my head.

QUESTION AND ANSWER

A Tale of Sutton Walls

Q.   Green rampart grassed, what have you seen and
heard?

A. Many a mourned deed and regretted word.

Q.   What the most mourned, the most regretted thing?

A. Ethelbert's murder under the great King.

Q.   Men marvel still at that . . . Why was it done?

A. Desire and wrath, two foemen of the Sun,
Because the great King's kin, Guthlac, of old,
Roved over seas for women, wine and gold,
Grew great and rich, and as his power failed,
Altered his ways, repented and bewailed;
Gave all he had to build what still abide,
The monkish cells at Croyland where he died;
Where his great bones, under the altar, heal
The sick and sore who call him as they kneel.
All-healing, is Saint Guthlac lying dead.
But Croyland was a fief of Ethelred,
Not in the Great King's realm; and the Great King
Counted those bones a spirit-saving thing.

He was of Guthlac's stock, his kinship claimed
Possession of such dust so greatly famed;
Total possession, for he planned to raise
Over that dust, a church that should amaze,
Stone-wrought and carven, painted, bright with gold,
Unparalleled where man inhabits mould,
Above which sweet-chimed bells should call and tell
Angels and men to join to conquer hell . . .
This, in his capital, unbuilt, but planned
To crown his life and glorify his land,
To bring from far and near the countless host
Who seek St Guthlac's help for flesh or ghost,
And make his capital, St Guthlac's Home,
The greatest Christian seat in Christendom.

But Ethelred, the Eastern King denied.
St Guthlac dead should stay where he had died.
No King in Christendom would lightly yield
So great a glory, so supreme a shield.

Q.   Ethelred owned no thing of greater worth:
        What King in Christendom held holier earth?

A. It seemed the keystone and the cornerstone
   Of all the structure Offa sought to own.
   Offa throughout his life had had the dream
   Of making this land One, himself supreme,
   With Guthlac, King and Saint, glory and guard.
   Throughout his life his struggle had been hard . . .

Think what he had achieved, while his name rang
Like steel smiting on iron with a clang:—
His battle trumpets blew across these Walls
Where now the skylarks sing and corncrake calls.
Kent was subdued and his; the south and west,
His blood-allies and partners manifest;
Northumbria his, by blood alliance firm;
Even wild Wales in friendship for a term,
He had achieved the Dyke that sets a bar
To all those children of the roving star;
The Kings of Italy and France would send
Legates and presents, proud to call him friend.
Could he but woo King Ethelred to grant
Saint Guthlac's dust, he had slight other want.

He thought, 'My girl, Elfrida, might persuade
That stubborn dog, she is a pretty maid;
Holy, as girls go, and as good a brown
As the cock partridge calling on the down.
She would persuade him, for she, too, desires
That holy dust to lay among his sires.
She with the hoard of Roman gold I won
When I killed Egbert under Ashendun,
She shall go plead and if her pleading fail
Words are but air, and iron may prevail.'

He called for Gwinbert, Counsellor and Lord,
His double-minded scoundrel and proved sword.
'Gwinbert, escort Elfrida, the Princess,
To Ethelred, the King at Outer Ness

I shall instruct her to what price to go
For this Saint's holy bones I covet so,
Ethelred's old, and beauty may persuade'.
Gwinbert prepared to take the royal maid,
Reflecting inly that it gave him chance
To give his statesman's schemes a furtherance.
He had received estates, with gold to boot,
To help Prince Eglan in his marriage suit.

Eglan, who planned, as Gwinbert knew alone,
To wed Elfrida and have Offa's throne.
Offa, all battle-hoary, could not last,
His wisdom and his luck were of the past,
With Offa dead, as dead he must be soon,
And Eglan King . . . the harp would be in tune.
Ethelred would refuse, as oft before,
Then Eglan, wedding as a prop the more,
Would come as balm on Offa's wounded pride.
With luck, Elfrida should be Eglan's bride.

The night before Elfrida started east
The holy well-spring under Malvern ceast;
Southward, by Woolhope, all a hillside shook;
Over the palace cawed a blood-red rook.
The chantry out at Pits was shaken down;
Three shrouded corpses swayed through Sutton Town
Singing old Roman songs of coming doom.
And then the rain fell, filling Lugg and Froom,
Till Leddon ran all red and Wye drowned more
Then ever her destruction drowned before.

And still the rain fell, fouling all the ways.
Elfrida's eastward ride took many days:
Through mire and flood she floundered, ill-bested,
When she reached Croyland, Ethelred was dead.

Then she must needs delay till the dead King
Took his last service at his burying,
And then delayed till Ethelbert, his heir,
After his crowning could receive her there.
Elfrida, Offa's Daughter, brown and glad
Looked then upon the planet's likeliest lad,
A youth so trim and true, so early-wise,
Each saw the other's soul with lovers' eyes,
Love that confounded errors and made plain
The way of wisdom, not to change again.
There, the two talked until the sun went down
And the round moon arose above the town.

There, still they talked, recovering from of old
Forgotten links of love of utter gold.
There they re-found the hopes so panted-for
And Gwinbert listened from behind the door.

Gwinbert took horse and galloped night and day
West, ever west, resolving what to say.

'This school-boy King to have Elfrida's hand?
Not while Sir Gwinbert and King Offa stand.
St Guthlac's ashes in exchange for her?
Not while Sir Gwinbert is the Minister.
Eglan shall have Elfrida: none but he.'

Westward he crossed, where Severn seeks the sea.
And west through grass by waters many-milled.
'This gay young cockerel shall be quickly killed'.
He galloped shouting, till he reached the King.

'Listen, Great Master, to this latest thing.
'King Ethelred is dead; his son succeeds.
A boy half monk, best fit for telling beads,
And this boy wooes your Daughter, the princess,
He rides to press his suiting, nothing less . . .

He offers a strange bargain: so, prepare . . .
You give Elfrida, making him your heir,
St Guthlac's bones will then be in your realm,
He says "a younger hand best suits a helm".
My stars, these eastern children have a nerve . . .
A school-boy, but a month a King, observe.
'And if King Offa should refuse,' he says,
King Offa cannot live for many days . . .
Offa shall hear my suit and give reply.'

'By thundering God,' said Offa, 'He shall die.
Which road's he take?'

                                'The south'.

                          'Go there and wait.
Meet him: delay him: till we close the gate.
Let not a word of his approach be known.
Say that the King will welcome him alone.
Come by the postern door, and there 'twere best
Say I permit no weapon on a guest.

So take his sword, and let him into Court,
Close the door after him and cut him short.
Black Mul shall help: then fling his bag of bones
There in the bogland at the stepping-stones.
Then, you and Mul, to Chester, to my son
And say what bride King Ethelbert has won.'

So, when the time arrived, this now green grass,
Then a walled city, felt the murder pass,
And the gate open to let Gwinbert go
Bearing a body to the Lugg below,
Then heard, and still remembers, the horse shoes
Splash the Lugg mud now crusht to redder ooze;
And so away, past Clee and Wrekin on,
To get away from what has never gone.

In the dark midnight while King Offa slept
Egmund and Britford the mid vigil kept;
They heard a woman sobbing on the stair,
A light approached, who could be moving there?
The hound at Britford's feet, with staring hide,
Quivered and whined and cowered terrified.
The wooden latch fell from the shaken door
A light displayed a woman weeping sore . . .
No earthly light, no moonlight, but the light
Of some deep purpose overcoming night.
So as the scared lads watched, the sobbing ceast:
It was Elfrida's spirit from the east . . .
'She is dead,' Britford whispered, 'and her ghost
Comes in farewell to all she loved the most.'

'Alas, I am not dead,' the shape replied.
'My love is dead with sword thrusts in his side.
'My love is murdered in the boggy place
By raddled Lugg with mud upon his face.
O Britford, Egmund, help my heart's distress,
I learned too late of Gwinbert's wickedness,
But my horse fell . . . I could not be in time
To quench my father's fury before crime . . .
But now, O save his body, I beseech.'

The two lads, rose, one spirit spoke in each.

The spirit, led into the summer dark . . .
No sentry called, no owl, nor did dogs bark,
All still the sleeping town, but the bright shape
Lit the still lane and bade the gateways gape.

Westward they went, till there, with wimpling tones
The summer Lugg lapped at the stepping-stones.
Elfrida pointed there and led the way,
To the tramped shallows where her lover lay.

'O Ethelbert,' she cried, 'I strove indeed . . .
But this, as Wisdom wills, has been decreed . . .
The promised end shall shortly come to pass,
Help Britford, Egmund, to this drier grass.'

They drew the body to the drier space,
They washed the mud from her dead lover's face,
Cleansed the dear hair and closed the startled eyes,
All life is spirit when a lover dies.

Elfrida's spirit said 'Mad John, the herd,
Will bring an oxcart ere the cocks have stirred.
Lay him upon the cart, Mad John will know
Ay, and the oxen, where he has to go.'

Even at this, that guiding shape of light
Dimmed into dawn-dim of the summer night.
She was not there but from a hedge near-by
A blackbird startled with his waking cry,
And from an elm above, a cuckoo tolled
His cheerful joy call, cuckoldy and cold.
Then, from the haystack of his summer bed,
Mad John, the herd, his cart and oxen led,
Singing 'You black-faced devils; Haw and Gee,
Go yonder, merry boys; then come to me.'

There the two squires laid the cart its load
And turned to town; the ox-cart took the road.
Singing, Mad John went, as the blackbird sings,
From some diviner sense of human things,
Until before him, there, on bush and spray,
Roses of all sorts seemed to bar his way,
Red, white and yellow, in such scent and glow
As naught but roses in such summers know,
Roses by this time sought by myriad bees
In the hot sunlight's honeyed secrecies.

Beyond the roses, in the green beyond,
The madman heard a tolling bell despond
And from the greenness, with a mourning hymn
The monastery monks came meeting him;

There, too, the convent nuns whom all folk bless,
And, with the nuns, Elfrida the Princess.

There was no need for given orders then.
Singing their hymn, the Abbot and his men
Came to the ox-cart censing what it bore,
Then, singing still, they turned towards the shore
Of Guardian Wye whose blessed channel closes
Black-mountained Rhondda from the land of roses.

Then, singing still, they turned into the fold,
Of Mary's minster church whose bell still tolled.
At the Church western door the ox-cart stayed.

'O Martyr, King and Saint,' the Bishop prayed,
'Be thou our help in Quire where we sing.'

The white Elfrida gave him back his ring.
She vowed herself to be a Nun thenceforth,
Gwinbert was killed in quarrel in the North
And Offa died, and his possessions merged
In other Kingdoms, as his rivals urged.
And Guthlac's dust remained in Croyland shrine.
Ethelbert's dust is with the bread and wine
Under the altar near his image still.
Apples and grasses cover Sutton Hill.

KING EDWARD THE CONFESSOR
AND HIS RING

Of all the Saints of whom we sing
As crowned and into glory gone,
Edward Confessor, Saint and King,
Loved best the loved Apostle John.

When any Church was consecrate
In Saint John's name, he bid me bear
Purses of gold exceeding great
And ride with him to give them there.

The wonder that I tell began
At just such blessing of a shrine.
I marked an outland beggar-man
Whose inward spirit seemed divine,

Who, when the sacring had been done,
Outside the Church, as the bells rang,
Stood silent, shining like the sun,
While the assembled quires sang.

Then, coming to the King, he cried:
'O King . . . a penny for my need.'
'The purse is empty,' I replied.
I showed it bare in very deed.

No widow's copper mite was in't.
The Kingly bounty would have made
Low water in the Royal Mint
He gave as Kingly nature bade.

'Stay, Friend, an instant,' said the King.
'No misery must ask in vain.
Brother, accept this finger-ring,
And may it raise your state again.'

It was his finger-ring, that bore
A table-emerald, so green
No May-time ever lovelier wore,
No June had ever lovelier seen.

Then the poor man with tears of grace
Blest gift and giver, deeply stirred.
He went, with light upon his face,
Singing thanksgiving for God's Word.

It fell, before the daffodil,
I went a pilgrimage abroad
Eastward, if such should be God's will
To tread the country of our Lord.

But I was wrecked midst foreign men,
And reached a city all alone
With temples of the Saracen
And minarets like spears of stone.

And fish-pools among orange groves
And sunny squares where fountains played,
And gateways where the camel droves
Burdened with spices, snarled and swayed.

And through the street, procession came.
The country's King, white-headed, crowned,
Who saw me, called me, asked my name
My faith, my home, and whither bound.

'Friend,' the King said, 'we've met before
Once, when you served the English King
Outside the newly-hallowed door
You saw him give this emerald ring.

I love your King: I welcome you.
You shall pass homeward over sea,
With Knights of mine for retinue,
And bear him back this ring from me.

And say that, six months to the day
I shall be there to bring him home
Where never darkness nor decay
Nor any sin or sorrow come.

And say that I, who tell you this,
Well know the praise he renders me.
I am St John, the Evangelist
Whom our Lord loved in Galilee.

And I, who, in the morning gloom
Peered in upon the chamber bare
On linen folded in a tomb,
I, John, shall be beside him there.'

Thus I returned: I gave the Ring
Back to its giver: told the tale
Of what was promised to the King
By one whose promise cannot fail.

And six months to the very day
Snow-eagles swept out of the sky
Calling the holy King away
To be with all that cannot die.

THE BURIED BRIDE
or
TRUE LOVE FINDS A WAY

After the wedding, all returned to feast.
The Mother of the Bride talked with the Priest.
'Yes . . . a good match . . . and Emily will soon
Forget her girlish crying for the moon.
It was but fancy that her heart should go
To Hugh, the child she played with, years ago.
That was absurd, and this she came to see,
And Hugh, of course, saw its absurdity.
When once a girl is married she is safe;
And women soon forget and cease to chafe.
But here is Lance: now, where is Emily?
She must have shed her wedding lacery.
Run, Janet, dear, and bid her hurry down,
Here is the wise Lord Provost of the Town.
Welcome, Lord Provost: yes, the sight was fair.
We are so very glad that you were there.
Yes, you shall see the Bride: she cannot be
More than a moment. Where is Emily?

JANET: 'O piteous, piteous; Emily is dead,
White, pulseless, breathless, lifeless on the bed.
As she foretold when I was with her there,
Lifting the bridal veilings from her hair,
She said, "Alas for my unhappy chance;

Heart-break to Hugh and misery to Lance,
And death to me, for I will not survive
Leaving my Hugh, the saddest soul alive.
And now I die," and even so she died,
In uttermost despair, not suicide.
She would not, could not, live, not having Hugh.'

LANCE: 'A pretty wedding feast you bring to me
But bring me to her: let me know the truth.'

There lay the maiden stricken in her youth,
White as her bridal flowers and as fair.
A silence shewed the guests were made aware.
They uttered formal grief and stole away.
And Lance, a widower on his marriage day,
Savage at what seemed trick, assumed a sorrow.
They laid her in the chancel till the morrow,
Then in the vault of Lance's ancestors
Buried her, scattered dust, and sealed the doors.

In the dark night, when all the city slept,
Hugh, who had loved her, to the chapel crept.
He broke the seals, hove back the doors and glid
Down to the vault where so much beauty hid.
There, setting down the light, he wrought, and raised
The plated plank on Emily and gazed.
There she lay lovely in her piteous peace.
'O happy darling to have found release,
Blessed release, from destiny too grim.
O better thus than ever slave to him,
To him to whom your dowry far outweighed
Your spirit's beauty, dear dead lovely maid.

Farewell, beloved Emily, but take
This lock of hair for Hugh your lover's sake.
You will be near me for what days remain
Before Death takes me and we meet again.
Farewell. Farewell.'
              Then, leaving the light burning,
He left the vault, the Church, and took the turning
Out of the parvise into the dark nooks
Where sometimes inn-signs creaked upon their hooks
And cats' eyes gleamed but all the town was dead.

The midnight bells told how the hours sped,
Then, as the chancel shewed a little light,
Emily's spirit wakened from her night.
She stirred, she roused, she saw the funeral scene,
Coffins and quartered shields of what had been.
She knew 'I have been buried: but they doubt . . .'
Conquering fear, she rose and tottered out
Into the Church, and thence back to her home.
There her devoted Janet saw her come
And called her Mother, others ran for Lance,
And all the town knew her deliverance . . .

But while some joyed, Lance, in much fury, said
'She's dead and buried: and her dowry's paid.
This is her wraith, not she, or sprig of hell
Dressed, for man's damning, in her body's shell.
I'll none of such damnation: gather faggot
Quick, ere she wrecks us, Bishop: burn the haggot.'

So might it have been done, for people then
Believed that devils took the forms of men
And many swore 'This thing in woman's shape
Is Satan's sending, let her not escape.
Burn her to ashes, brothers: she's a witch.'

So, swift, they came with faggots, fire, pitch
Powder, and chains, and in the market-square
Drove in a stake and laid the pyre fair,
Then, yelling, led by Lance, they ran to fetch
Their victim from her home to burn the wretch.
But now the Provost and his men appeared.
'Back, you,' he cried, 'and let the place be cleared.
Back; all of you; upon your peril; back.'

But hot blood has the pleasure of attack,
And hate its minute's joy at any cost.
So, here, the riot disobeyed and lost.
And in the mellay, Lance, flung from his horse
And dragged by stirrup was a trampled corse
Kicked out of semblance when they cut the thong.

So Destiny and death annulled the wrong
Wrought by the plotting mind to gather gain.
Emily's shroud and coffin served again
That very night, for Lance, and there he lies.
His spirit wanders somewhere growing wise,
Or so I hope, before another chance.
And Emily, forever quit of Lance,
Gave her dead lord's possessions as seemed due.

Then in most happy time she married Hugh.

169

JOHN GRIMALDI
or
THE SAILOR'S RETURN

Not all forgotten yet in London Town
Is Joe Grimaldi, once the famous Clown.
Though vanished from the Stage these many moons
Men know what songs he sang, if not the tunes.
Some hint or shadow of his figure lingers
In ancient prints of pits and clowns and singers.
And many know he played the tragic part
Of making merry with a broken heart.

Who was this darling of that distant age?
An actor's son, born almost on the stage.
Theatre-drawn with every breath he drew.
(He played a monkey's part ere he was two)
He, and his younger brother John, were both
Theatre-doomed, Joe willingly, John loth.
Birth-doomed, to drag through childhood's bitter days
On scanty bread from tiny parts in plays,
Joe, glad, however bitter it might be,
John, loathing all, and longing for the sea.

John, being seven, brighter hopes began;
A berth was found him in an Indiaman,
His kit was given and aboard he went,
Bound for the Spice Isles of the Orient

Or so he hoped, but found a long delay
Of toil in port ere getting under way.
Toil all unwelcome to a tiny boy
Expecting liberty and sailor's joy
And finding thraldom and unwelcome cheer
Salt, dark and dirty in a cable-tier
With none to teach him, save by kick and blow,
The unknown art he was supposed to know.

There, as he sorrowed, sailor-sick and sad,
Another prospect opened to the lad.
A near-by frigate had command to sail
Next day at dawn should wind and tide avail.
Surely, in her, he would at once achieve
The grand, free life of men who cannot grieve,
Who sail upon white wings as Neptune's sons
Annihilating England's foes with guns;

Then, rich with prize, return in glory, singing,
Setting the Minster bells of England ringing . . .
Surely, in her . . .
                    Thus little boys of seven
Dream of the life at sea as life in Heaven.
So, in the dusk, this little John, stripped bare
And left his Indiaman at anchor there,
And swam, all naked, to the frigate's side,
To volunteer where no-one was denied.
But to what tests they put him, and what rank
He climbed to in that peril of sea-plank,
Is all unknown, his person disappears,
No word of him is heard for fourteen years.

Meanwhile his brother Joe, by slow degrees
Learned upon jealous stages how to please,
Learned all the craft, and met with John again,
While playing comedy in Drury Lane.
While in the wings and waiting for his cue
A man said 'Joe, some people ask for you.
Two men: they wait below, till you are free.'

Thither Joe went; gay sprigs they seemed to be,
Elegant youths, and strangers both, he thought.
But one most pressingly his notice caught,
Showing a tiny scar upon his chest,
It was John's self, his brother manifest,
Returned, and rich, for as he made avow
'I have six hundred pounds upon me now.'
'John there is danger laying such facts bare.'
'Sailors despise all danger everywhere.'
'In town, they should not; but, I must not stay.
Come to the Green Room till we end the play.
Wroughton is there, who fitted you for sea.'

Then John's companion uttered hastily,
'I'll call for you tomorrow, John, at ten.'
This John confirmed, the friend departed then.
It was remembered later, none had heard
Aught of this friend, no name, nor other word,
Nor noticed him, save that, like John, he bore
Gear ready-made, as one just come ashore.
Blue coat, white waistcoat, and a gold-topped cane,
Thus geared, he left and never came again.

172

Within the Green Room, John made many friends,
Joe came and went at scene and curtain ends;
But when the play was over Joe was free.
'John, when I've changed, you must come home with me.'
And here he told of Mother, Wife and home,
And what a joy it was that John had come,
To share their life: and asked, How long ago
John had reached town.
                                   'Two hours' time, or so . . .
Time just to dine and come to Drury Lane.'
'When I have changed I'll take you home again.'
And here he named the number and the street.
Now I will change: wait here until we meet.'

Leaving John there, Joe hurried off to change.
But John's arrival had made all seem strange,
All marvellous, miraculous, undreamed . . .
Changing his clothes took longer than he deemed.
But having dressed, an actor hailed him thus:
'Ah, Joe, what fun for you and all of us . . .
Your brother's on the stage, that lively blade . . .
He says you've been much longer than you said.'

John was not on the stage; a man said, 'No . . .
I saw him here not twenty ticks ago . . .
He went towards the stage-door, down the stair.'
Joe hurried thither, but John was not there.
'Went out a minute since,' the porter cried,
'No, not so much: he must be just outside . . .'
But no John showed in the dim lamp-lit lane,
No John at all was there, so much was plain.

173

'Of course,' Joe cried, 'there where the windows glow . . .
The Bowlbys live: he knew them long ago.
Young Bowlby was his friend: he's calling there.'
Thither they went, but found the covert bare.
'Yes. John was here not half a minute past!'
Old Bowlby said, 'That's where I saw him last
Going to Duke Street, just beyond the bend.'
'Baily's,' said Joe, 'Our landlord, then, and friend.
He's gone to Baily's. On, to Baily's all.

Blank windows watched the night from Baily's wall . . .
Joe knocked and rang: but nobody replied.
At last an upper window opened wide.
A maid put head out 'As I said before . . .
He's not at home . . . stop knocking at the door.'
            'Who's not at home?'
                      'Why, Mr Baily, sir.'

Within the darkened house, there came a stir,
A light, the maid descended, and unchained.
'A man came knocking here, Sir,' she explained
Rousing the street, Sir, not a minute past.
Our Mr Baily left here Friday last . . .
Going to Hungerford, out Berkshire way . . .
I told the man, Sir, and he went away.
And when you knocked, I thought he'd come again.
From up above I could not see him plain.
Only his waistcoat white . . .'

                  'Well . . . it was John.
He came to look-up Baily and has gone . . .
Gone to the theatre, no doubt, for me.

Back to the theatre, then, hurriedly.'
Joe thanked the girl, and hurriedly returned.

The theatre was shut, though light still burned,
Men, closing-down, unbolted to the knock.
No-one had entered since they turned the lock,
John was not there, had never come again.
'He has gone home to Mother, it is plain.'
Joe said, 'I told him the address; he's there.'
So, swiftly, by still street and empty square,
By cats and watchman's braziers, and odd light,
Late cart or passer, of a town at night,
He hurried home, and knocked, and was let in.

Strangeness had shewn; now tragedies begin.
Joe found his Mother pale, and asked in doubt,
'Has anybody called, since I went out?'
'No-one . . . Who should have called?'
                    'Your son, John, home.'
The Mother swooned; alas, no John had come,
And though she hoped the night through, did not come.

But John's companion (Joe remembered, then)
Had clearly said 'I'll call for you at ten.'
So, before ten, Joe was on watch again
In and about the doors of Drury Lane
But neither John nor friend th' appointment kept.

Joe and his Mother waited, watched and wept.
Asked, sought, entreated, but they never heard
Of brother John again one helpful word.

No littlest trace of him was ever found.
By many means Death brings us to the ground,
But where or by what means Joe's brother died
None came to know, though many seekers tried.
The tiny glimpse of one who knocked by night
Caught by the maid, the half-seen glimpse of white,
Remained the last glimpse seen of brother John.
From darkness come and into darkness gone.

Some thought a press-gang hurried him aboard
A ship at point to sail to death abroad.
Some, that a tempter lured him into hold
Near Drury Lane, and killed him for his gold.
Some, that the unknown friend had plotted this.
Cities and Night hide many mysteries.

Some have imagined that he came to knock
His Mother's door and begged her to unlock.
Calling himself 'Your John, returned from sea' . . .
That she refused, a lone, weak woman she . . .
There, in an unlit suburb, late at night . . .
That, then, at her refusal, in despite,
He had abandoned every thought of home,
And turned to that unknown whence he had come.

Some ask, if that that Drury Lane perceived
Were, truly, living man, as men believed,
Not ghost or phantom of John newly dead
Fulfilling hope long unaccomplishéd,
Through thwarting Death upon fulfilment's brink?
Longing for home is stronger than men think

And after fourteen years of sea, at war,
Starved of all tenderness men hunger for,
The longing may have focused to such flame
That it out-struggled Death and overcame
Allowing the loosed soul to have her will.

So some have wondered, as they wonder still.
The answer to the problem no man knows.
The hearts that ached have finished now with woes.

A WORD WITH SIR FRANCIS DRAKE
DURING HIS
LAST NIGHT IN LONDON

1595

Scene: A room at night. SIR FRANCIS DRAKE *writing. One knocks.*

DRAKE: Come in. (TIRROLD *enters.*)
                                        What now?

TIRROLD: You won't remember me,
　　But, Sir, I had to see you . . .

DRAKE: Let me see . . .
　　You were aboard . . . not Christopher . . . Wait yet.
　　Frank, then, Frank Tirrold, if I don't forget.
　　Weren't you my fiddler in the *Golden Hind*?

TIRROLD: O Sir . . . that you should keep me still in mind.

DRAKE: I don't forget old shipmates. Come, sit down.
　　Sit, man: what brings you into London Town?
　　Prosperity, it seems: do you still play?

TIRROLD: Yes, and make others sing, this many a day.
　　I'm music-master in the play-house there.

178

DRAKE: We were great fellows in the days that were.
A score, perhaps, still living, sprinkled round,
Somehow un-hanged, and somehow never drowned.
Shall we away, and round the world agen?

TIRROLD: Sir, you have done enough for twenty men.
For me, once round will serve for twenty lives.
While dry land stands and offers gaols and gyves.
And prison-chains and iron bars and locks,
I'll have no more of running upon rocks,
Eight thousand miles from home: once serves for me.

DRAKE: To each, his lot: my Fortune is the sea.
We were near death that day upon the reef.

TIRROLD: We'd have met death there with a lesser chief.
And many other days, too, west and east.
Glory is like a coronation feast
It suits the ruler, not the foremast hand.

Sir . . . one small thing I cannot understand . . .
The book there is, describing what betid
The wide world round, the wonders that you did,
It tells of snowfall in that western bay
Where we careened ere going west away.
The white-cliffed harbour that you made us call
New Albion . . . we had no snow at all.

DRAKE: None, Frank, the stories of the snow are lies,
Or facts misplaced or truths in some disguise,
Just facts and truths divulged with altered dates
From my account of the Magellan Straits.

Lies to deceive the Spaniards and to scare
All greedy dons from trying settling there.
They like the sun.

TIRROLD: But, Sir, no falsehood told
    Will frighten any man from seeking gold.
    Then; they have captured some of us and learned
    The truth, by torture, ere they hanged or burned.

DRAKE: The falsehood served, they never took the land . . .
    That unsailed sea still beats upon its sand.
    Nor have we taken it, this weary while.
    Yet, standing there, so many a thousand mile
    From England, thinking what a land we held,
    I tell you, Master Tirrold, my heart swelled.

    You saw it, too, the miracles that lay
    Twelve hundred miles from Acapulco Bay . . .
    A port beyond all praise for every good
    Shelter, careenage, safety, water, food.
    Think of those herds of deer; recall to mind
    The plains free-warrened with the coney kind,
    The fruits on tree and bush, the myriad fish,
    In sea or brook, each one a royal dish.
    Seals on the rocks, or roaring, in seas breaking,
    The trees, those miracles, that set us aching
    To build great ships from such eternal wood.
    Then both the climate and the soil so good,
    That wild grapes grew, so excellent they were.

Tirrold, I longed to have the English there.
Man . . . we had proved that there must ever be
A South-West Passage to the Southern Sea . . .
The Spaniards never guessed it but we found it.
That great America has water round it.

TIRROLD: Fierce water, too; and wind: a two months trip,
　　　With danger every day to man and ship.

DRAKE: All seas are danger, but it stands to reason
　　　Since all known waters have a summer season,
　　　In some such season, once in every year,
　　　All ships could stand the buffet and pass clear.
　　　Five hundred men, as strong as we, could seize
　　　That whole West Coast, as we did, and with ease,
　　　And smash King Philip's empire into dust.

　　　Then, based upon that harbour with our ships
　　　They'd put his eastern empire in eclipse.

TIRROLD: You mean, that we might settle there . . . and
　　　stay?

DRAKE: I hoped so, Tirrold, on that distant day.
　　　I hoped that England's Queen might see it so . . .

TIRROLD: Sir, we were young men with you, yet you know
　　　Whether we loved that hell at the world's ends,
　　　Twelve thousand salt-sea miles from home and friends.
　　　We just endured it, but no tongue can say
　　　Our agonies of hope to get away.

Only devotion to you and the thought
Of home at last, preserved us as we wrought.
We were scarce sane; but what would settlers be?
Then, Sir, the Indians, how could they agree?
No western Indian loves to share his land.
The white men take it with the iron hand . . .
And, Sir, those Indians were no common foes.
No two of us could wrestle one of those.

DRAKE: They were our friends: they mourned us when we
    sailed.
It was my hope for England, but it failed.
It is this changeful England's tidal air,
It quenched the light that shone so starry there.
We long for Spain's destruction; yet endure
All things from Spain, and never seek the cure.

By Fortune and her Star, I tell you plain,
Fortune and I could thrice have ruined Spain;
Crumpled her up, like some false letter read,
And flung her to her place among the dead.
Fortune and I together would have done
Matters not often seen beneath the sun.

First, at St Johns, where I'd have held my ground,
Trusting no Spaniard, even if they drowned.
We were at war there, we could no more trust
The Spaniards there than angry asps in dust.
John feared to sink their fleet, yet all the same
What else did John do when the Armada came?

182

We had to sink it some time; why not then,
Saving those hundreds of our countrymen
Then murdered by the dogs whom we had spared?

That was the first great chance, had Hawkins dared.

Then, the next chance, a bullet struck me down
Just as I won their famous treasure-town,
And had within my hand all Spain's estate,
Silver and gold in bars, eight thousand weight.

Then, at New Albion, what a way was showed,
But asses ever choose the thistly road,
And so the Armada came . . .
                              What drove it hence?
Fortune our friend: not gunpowder and sense.

And now tomorrow I am off again
For yet another piece-meal thrust at Spain.
But this time, after twenty years of me,
Spain may have learned more common sense than we;
Spain, not myself, may spring surprises now.

God's way is wondrous and to That I bow.

The die is cast; tomorrow I'll be gone.

TIRROLD: To do new deeds for men to wonder on.

DRAKE: Youth does the wonders: yet I hope to try.
        Now, Frank, farewell: good Fortune and goodbye.

TIRROLD: To you, all Fortune. I beseech the Lord
To bring you home, with Spanish gold aboard.

But one thing, Sir, those Indians in the Bay
The red New Albion Indians west away . . .

Good Master Chaplain said that he had learned
That they believed we were their dead returned.
I find no Scripture text to warrant this . . .
But can it be that such a land there is?
A land, far west, where the beloved dead
Live, plying other tasks for other bread . . .
To whom we might give thanks or make amends.
Our Mothers, or our lovers, or our friends?

DRAKE: No mortal knows God's ends, nor the world's ends.
Good Master Chaplain (as you call him) might
Have shed you some such darkness from his night:
I cannot: being a sailor, in command.

But this I'll say . . . If I could understand
That such a country lies in any sea
And what its bearing is, and its degree,
I would set forth, and find, and search it through,
For just two men, or either of the two,
Enriquez, once the Viceroy at St Johns,
And Admiral Luxan, liars both and dons.

Could I find both, my sword against the pair,
I'd fight the two, and beat, and hang them there,
On one good rope on which I might depend.

The death I dealt would be their utter end.
They'd live no longer in their happy isle.

And after that, why, Death would be worth while.

But no such Fortune has been, nor will be.
Spain's still the rock and I the assaulting sea.
Again, all happy fortune and good cheer.
If I return with Fortune you shall hear.

LINES
ON THE SHIPWRECK OF
ADMIRAL SIR CLOUDESLEY SHOVELL,
IN
OCTOBER, 1707,
ON THE ROCKS SOMETIMES CALLED
'THE BISHOP AND HIS CLERKS'

Fog covered all the great Fleet homeward bound,
No sights for days, all groping up by sound,
And, finding Soundings, all were well aware
How thick with hidden Death those waters were.

So, in no gleam of any light, they lay
With topsails furled, that grim October day,
With senses strained to learn what lay ahead
But nothing bringing knowledge save the lead,
And thus, unsurely, slowly brought to hand
Could but repeat, that they were nearing land.

There the divisions of the power heaved,
In the seas' menace, while the tackles grieved,
The timbers cried their culminating creak,
And great drops dripped on men afraid to speak,
The while they listened, bell by weary bell,
For sight or sound of something that would tell.
But no sign came, save ship-sign dim or clear
From ship on ship, all threatened and all near.

Where were they, then? All wondered, but none knew
What Death lay hidden, nor how near it drew,
But all the squadron's masters knew at least
A seaman's graveyard lay to north and east
Too near for quiet and too grim to chance,
The Scilly Isles, those rocks of old romance.
And yet, no sound of breakers could be heard
Where Death on sentry challenged for the Word.
No strike of clock, or church-bell from the shore,
Just fog, astern, alongside, and afore.
And sometimes timing-cries, as seamen hauled
Or boatswains' pipes, or hails, or orders called.

Such dangers as they knew that autumn day
Came from themselves, slow-heaving, without way.
For sometimes, with wild cries and lantern-flash,
Ships would heave near to some expected crash,
And crews make tumult, bells and drums and guns,
Blinding the comers' eyes with malisons,
Till, dripping in slow heave, with creak of strain,
The threat withdrew into the fog again.

So the day passed, until a livelier breath
Lifted the darkness of that fog of death,
And there, ahead, afar, a welcome sight,
Seen, recognised by all, St Agnes' Light. . .
Surety at last: the Flag, by guns and hail
Bade the Fleet eastward under easy sail.

So, with a creaking of great gear, they turned
And fog recovered where the light had burned,

187   N

But it had beaconed that the course was clear,
So mainsails filled and hearts abandoned fear.
But forty miles, by midnight at the most,
And then, Land's End, and then, the Cornish Coast,
The Lizard before dawn, and then, ahead,
The distant Start, the Devon ploughland red.
Men of the forenoon watch could surely say
'We'll sight the Rame Head before close of day.'
And some, more bold, would be by wager bound
The fleet would pass next night in Plymouth Sound,
Land-locked, at ease, in station, snugly moored,
The sails furled, the yards squared, the guns secured.
And boats alongside peddling fruit and bread.
And church chimes telling how the hours sped.

Thus, in the night, those users of the sea
Talked in their prison of their being free,
Knowing, the while, that every lift and 'scend
Brought them a ship's length nearer to Land's End.
Not knowing then that unseen currents streamed
Setting them ever north of where they deemed.
A seaman's graveyard hedges England's shores,
And Fortune rules, and Death has many doors.

All the great fleet the starless midnight strode,
Crushing the blackness into gleams that glowed,
Seeing at whiles (when aught they might discern)
A space ahead, the Admiral's lanterns burn
Where like sea-monsters gleaming at the gorge,
The *Association* led, with the *St George*.

Who shall be sure what wind they had, what speed,
What sight or sound of warning to take heed,
What flash or roar of breakers, or intense
Shocking fierce pang of danger touching sense?

Suddenly, dead ahead, the seamen saw
Rocks among billows in a hell of awe,
No time for backing yards or changing helm,
Time but to signal lest the fleet o'erwhelm,
So lights, flares, guns, despite the terror, blazed.
The *Association* struck, the *St George* grazed,
Three minutes made the flagship broken plank,
Within four minutes of the crash she sank.
The men in the *St George*, themselves swept clear,
Saw suddenly her lanterns disappear.
The *Eagle* and the *Romney*, following close
Struck, staved, and sundered whence they never rose.
The *Firebrand* went down, and but one man
Of these lost ships was saved: the *Royal Anne*
Struck and broke clear, her quarter railings gone.
The *Phoenix* struck, with loss, but floated on.

Thus in five minutes of blind death and scare
Two thousand seamen ceased to breathe the air
And drifted for the gulls or sank below
To unlit silence where the congers go.
A quarter of the fleet gone, but the rest

Saved as Fate willed by being further west
Or by the lucky cannon that gave guide
Through the last conscious act of those who died,

Men in the Flagship, who from top or deck
Fired at once to save the Fleet from wreck,
And then, an instant later, felt the ship
Collapsing, fling salt death upon their lip,
And one wild instant's terror bringing peace.

One seaman only did the sea release
From sudden death when the two thousand drowned.
Three days thereafter he was seen and found
Alive, upon Hellweather Rock, and saved.

Thus, the returning battleships were staved
Upon the Bishops and the Gilstones grim
Where now the seaman's beacons welcome him,
The first light seen, the last light dropped astern
In hopeful sailing or in glad return.

H.M.S. *CALLIOPE*
IN THE HURRICANE,
IN APIA BAY, SAMOA,
MARCH 16TH 1889

Into full hurricane the wind increased
Blasting the warships in Apia Bay.
Aboard the ship *Calliope* men deemed
Their anchors dragged: they longed for coming day.
In rain and flying spume the norther screamed,
Yelling like all the hounds of hell released
The reefs looked nearer when the lightnings gleamed
The terror that was morning shewed how near.

Reefs hard at hand and doomed ships dragging drear.
Calliope, sea-streaming like a sluice,
Now battened down against the appalling sea.
Then her fore-yard snapped lashings and broke loose,
And swung there like a devil having glee,
Threatening mast and ship: a thing of fear.
Brave seamen made it let its swinging be.
Then Death himself showed betwixt ship and shore.

Death's very self, wide-opening his door,
The anchors useless and the breakers close,
The ship *Vandalia*, helpless, dead ahead,
And now, in sudden sheer, the *Olga* rose,
Her bowsprit struck the foreyard as she sped,

It thrust her off a living instant more,
Or, in collision, both ships had been dead,
Rammed, one or both, and sunk, with none to tell.

Then, on *Calliope*, a marvel fell:
The vast *Vandalia* swung beneath her bow
Lifting her, by the bowsprit, as she rolled,
Snapping its gear, and yet, men knew not how,
Although the very blood of all ran cold
Then rolled away again and all was well,
The released bowsprit fell back as of old,
The ships swung clear: Life gave an instant's grace.

Still, the *Calliope* had Death in face,
The reef three yards astern, in surf past telling;
The helpless *Olga* swinging at her side;
The air all devils from all hell rebelling;
Ahead, *Vandalia*, poised to re-collide;
No anchor holding, and of lull no trace,
Yet half one little instant to decide,
Whether to stay, or struggle to go out.

One little hope shone in that death of doubt:
To slip the cable and to steam to sea,
Backing a yard, to clear *Vandalia*'s stern,
Missing the reef, and her (if that might be);
Then, if the engines told, the luck might turn;
Then, if the gear held and their hearts were stout,
And the *Olga* spared them, they might live and learn.
Kane gave command for 'every pound of steam'.

Who has not suffered anguish in a dream,
Devil or Death at hand, at point to spring,
The hooded cobra poised, the axe uplifted,
And gasped for dread of what a gasp might bring?
The ship, her cable slipped, an instant drifted
She paused betwixt the fury and the scream,
In utmost strain, yet seemingly unshifted.
With two ships dragging helpless in her way.

The three seemed bound for Death in Dead Man's Bay,
Above the tempest's yell rose the surf's thunder.
The engines beat, and yet the ship stood still.
Then the *Vandalia* surged to put her under.
Stern-on, she weltered, like a moving hill,
Coming to swamp what could not get away.
Then, as the two ships merged, they rolled asunder,
The *Olga* surged alongside, but swept clear.

Slowly, in tensest strain on all the gear,
The ship *Calliope* began her crawl,
Deluging bow and stern, yet making head.
And now the flagship *Trenton* lay in sprawl,
Swinging across the channel, sore-bested.
Her rudder broken, that she could not steer
Her engine-room all swamped, her fires dead,
A barrier to the pathway to the sea.

She swung athwart-hawse the *Calliope*,
This way and that as the confused sea bade,
Barely a length betwixt her and the reef
Almost a wreck and sorely needing aid.

But all heroic effort stifles grief,
Her seamen saw their sister of the sea,
(As at a death the star of a belief,)
They manned the *Trenton*'s side and cheered and cheered.

Gladly our seamen answered as they neared;
In that blind peril brave heart answered heart,
In that mad channel between reef and ship
The touch of Fortune's hand kept death apart.
The shears that bring destruction did not clip.
In the blind storm the *Trenton* disappeared.
Calliope, all ocean at her lip,
Strode on to open sea in the gale's roaring.

ON PILOTS

Pilots, those unknown beings, who remove
All ships and seamen from the homes of love,
Yet, still unknown, at long last, cheer the sight,
Like the first sounding or the Bishop Light,
And bring them home, to the desired place.

O memory, praise them, before Death efface.

Many have watched the Channel Pilot leave
His plunging charge at setting-in of eve,
Have heard his cry of 'Letters for ashore',
While the unsheeted topsails slat and roar,
He, gathering letters, hurrying good-byes,
Leaps to his boat on some well-taken rise,
And so away, while she, (his charge) again
Bows to blue water to the south of Spain.

O, to how many, nearing coast or port,
On some keel-trodden way of ship-resort,
The Pilot-Schooner has appeared, displaying
Skill in the sea-arts beyond mortal telling;
Some daughter of the pine-woods near the sea,
Each timber shaped by him who felled the tree,
On Massachusetts' coast, or colder Maine.

There the sweet sea-horse leant against the rein;
She with a feather whitening at her lip,
Sure as a sea-gull sidling to her ship,
And then away, upon another quest,
A swimming sea-bird seemingly at rest,
One with the water, yet the water's Queen.

Can the old Hoogli pilots still be seen?
The Brig-Men, studying the hourly change
Of depth, of current-speed, of current-range,
Of shoals becoming deeps; of deeps that filled
(No warning given), as the River willed;
Of sands engulfing any ship that struck,
In depthless unplumbed squotulence of muck,
Leaving but eddies wrinkling under sky,
Wrinkling away, with bodies floating by?

They held half England's shipping in their hands,
Both up and down, and saved it from the sands.
Where pilots now have engines that prevail,
Those pilots handled charges under sail.
Often, in channels without room to turn,
They sailed them in and backed them in astern,
And plucked them outward on the sailing day.

Power has given man an easier way
These many years, but we should keep in mind
When weakness was and every way was blind,
When England's shipping had no mark to bless
Between Old London Bridge and Dungeness,

When all that seamen's threat had no defence
Save common sense and too uncommon sense;
When the young Nelson, still a growing boy,
Learned to be pilot groping in a hoy.

No easy task for lads in such a school,
To take a ship in charge in London Pool,
To seize the ebb, and pull her from the herd:
Perhaps at quiet dawn when no wind stirred,
To tide her down, her only strength an oar,
Tugged, to change course, twixt Wapping and the Nore.
So, loitering down, with fifty loitering down,
The gallows-beaconed road from London town,
Nearing collision, but by luck and skill
Just scraping clear as clever pilots will,
Catching a moment's gust, an instant's chance,
By doing hand and understanding glance.

Then, perhaps, drifting into fog not knowing
What lay ahead, or near, but keeping going
The instinct, ear, and scent alike at strain
For some least hint that made the matter plain;
Perhaps a cock-crow from a Kentish Farm,
(Even a mooing cow has given alarm)
Or whiff from hayfield, lime-kiln, bonfire-smoke,
Each, coming when it did, a voice that spoke.

He who has drifted thus in fogs, unseeing,
Has touched his spirit's unseen Greater Being.

197

Was there not once (some generations since)
An invitation from a foreign Prince
Sent to an English Fleet to make a stay
In some close harbour for Regatta Day?
Himself, the foreign Prince, would pilot all,
Proud, in his yacht, lest dangers should befall,
He, the land's Prince, would greatly, kindly, lead
To that snug cove, the anchorage decreed.

Then, as the teller told, a fog ensued,
Fog in her unity of solitude,
Dumb as old Death, save where the bell-buoys tossed
Their desolate lamentings of things lost.
Fog covered land and water, beast and man,
Blurring both anchorage and royal plan.
'So,' the Prince said, 'we cannot steam today,
To pilot-in the English to the bay.
Well . . . they must wait . . . the fog will lift anon.'

A night went by; a struggling sunbeam shone,
Or seemed to shine: upon a little wind,
Hardly a breath, the nulling dimness thinned,
A summer brightness shone on all the bay.
There in the cove appointed, our fleet lay,
Anchored, aligned, in order, distance kept,
Self-piloted through fog while landsmen slept.

There comes a memory from the long-since seen;
The *Waterwitch*, the Pilot's barquentine,
In summer sunset gliding like a ghost
Under all sail along the English coast.

Who did not envy those aboard her, then,
The lads there training to be pilot-men
Whose books were Nature's doings, seamen's guides,
Shallows and depths, sea-currents, sets and tides;
Rocks breaking and rocks hidden, where the tint
Upon the water's surface gave the hint;
And all that wisdom gathered from the lead
When sudden fog engulfed what lay ahead;
Their life's communion with the Greater Mind
That told the courses when the way was blind;
The acute senses that receive and fuse
At once, the fifty signs to one of use?
What happier life for youth, than to engage
To spend a twelvemonth learning pilotage?

'By God and guess,' the seaman's proverb said,
So are paths found, where paths were never made.
By thought's intensity transcending thought,
The way is found, the ship to safety brought,
Or sent away, with every hope to thrive
Breasting blue water like a thing alive.

THE STRANGE CASE OF
CAPTAIN BARNABY

There seems to be no doubt that, in or about the year 1687, a Mrs Booty, the widow of a brewer, caused the trial of Captain Barnaby in the Court of King's Bench, 'in a Suit of £1,000 damages', for the defamation of her late husband's character, by the repetition of the tale told here.

The case was heard before the Chief Justice, Herbert, and three Judges, Wythens, Holloway and Wright.

Members of the crews of three small ships swore that they had seen Mr Booty driven into a fiery furnace on the island of Stromboli at 3.14 p.m. on the previous 15 May, as they rested ashore there, after killing curlews for sea-store.

The Chief Justice declared that such testimony could not be doubted, and that they had seen Mr Booty, however strange and awful the tale might seem: Mrs Booty therefore lost her case.

We were bound home, when, on the second day
We raised the Fiery island and drew near.
We marked one glowing cranny smoking gray,
But all else glittered green and promised cheer.
The brooks were sparkling, and the birds in air
Uncountable as snow-flakes and as lovely.

So, being short of water and of meat,
I bade my consorts anchor, and then land.
We filled the barrels of our little fleet,
Then in a long line forming, gun in hand,

We walked the grass and shot the grey sea-geese,
The great St Martin's plovers and sea-curlews.

Enough, for all three ships, to last us in.
At the grass-edge, I bade the shooting cease.
But then we saw a most strange game begin.
Prone in the grass we watched it at our ease.
A negro and a white seemed playing tag
Down on the sea-beach where the boats were lying.

I cannot call to mind who saw them first,
But some one called 'Who are they? None of ours.'
As all men know, the island is accurst,
Unvisited except in daylight hours.
No other ship than ours rode the bay,
Yet here two strangers played at Snap and Dodger.

We were two hundred yards at least away.
Our keepers of the boats were watching, too.
The couple dodged the east side of the bay.
And one thing in the game we swiftly knew:
The black was bent on driving him to us,
The white one tried to pass him and get eastward.

Now we, to westward, lay below the scree
Above which, in the rock, the cranny glowed
Red, sometimes, putting colour on the sea,
Then dimming into dusk as the fumes flowed.
We heard our boatmen hail them: no reply
Came from the two intent upon their dodging.

The next thing that we noticed was the speed,
The unusual speed, with which the negro ran,
Not only swift, but tireless, indeed
A leopard or a greyhound of a man,
And every burst or effort to get by
  Was headed back, towards us, nearer, nearer.

Mostly, the white man's face was to the east;
We saw the black face better, clear-cut, lean,
Something betwixt an Arab and a priest
With every faculty intently keen.
He wore black runners' shorts, close to the skin
And never wild-cat watched his quarry better.

And then, we marvelled that the dodgers paid
No heed whatever to us twenty men
Prone on the grass, watching the game they played:
We were as accidents beyond their ken,
They were intent upon an unknown game
On which (we felt assured) big stakes depended.

Then, as they neared, the white man's figure seemed
Familiar, somehow, to me, shape and pose
Perhaps some recollection of dream dreamed.
Then suddenly (by this time they were close)
I saw his face, and cried 'For the sea's sake
Why . . . this is Mr B, my next-door neighbour.'

Then both my mates, and others of my crew
Agreed 'Old Mr B, marine-purveyor,'
A not too honest one, as well we knew

For many a horse-shoe lay in many a layer
Of skin and bone purveyed by him as beef.
We hailed him: 'Mr B . . .' he took no notice.

None, but he turned, not seeing us, not knowing,
Only exhausted, and the black one sprang
Gripped him and carried to the cranny glowing,
Which opened red and took them with a clang,
One instant they glowed red, then the rocks clashed;
The smoke blew clear: the rock face bore no cranny.

Then, truly, we were on our feet, aghast.
What had we seen but someone borne to hell
Dragged to the doom of flames that ever last
One whom we all had seen and some knew well.
The cranny had closed-to upon the pair
A little smoke curled upward from the rock-face.

We crept toward the rock, hot to the feet,
Plainly appalling heat was just within . . .
And growlings of great powers shook the heat;
We were at Hell, the punishment of sin.
White-faced, without a word we took our loads
Back to the boats, and so aboard, for England.

So, reaching home, I asked for Mr B.
Friends, he had died that very hour and day
When we had watched him hunted by the sea
Into Hell's door a thousand miles away.
Died in distress, they said, for things ill done.
Had what we seen been his eternal sentence?

Well . . . our tale spread, that we had seen him borne
Into Hell fire by a thing of Hell,
And Mrs. B. soon heard, you may be sworn.
As you suppose, she did not take it well.
She heard a Captain's wife repeat the tale
And sued her, straight, for slandering her husband.

Perhaps the Captain's Wife had touched the tale:
I know not, but the widow's case was brought
With all hands summoned and forbid to sail
And nothing talked of more and little thought.
Till there we were a-kissing Books in court
Before Lord Justice and the other Judges.

Mind, thirty-five of us had seen the pair,
Those in the ships, those in the boats, and we
And each one of these twenty last could swear
That beyond doubt the white was Mr B . . .
His hair, his venerable look, his eyes . . .
A mark, where a dog bit him, on his knuckles.

So, having heard, the Lord Chief Justice spoke.
'No stranger case has ever yet been tried.
What seemed at first an ill-intentioned joke
Stands, now, unique, no precedent to guide:
You have heard twenty men confirm the fact.
This was no fiction, but a witnessed act.
However strange, however out of reason,

Beyond all doubt, they tell of what they saw,
A thing most terrible, a granted sight
Of Justice done by an eternal law
That without statute ministers the right.
This the condemning Justice let them see
For purpose not revealed, but surely righteous.

The case before us fails.'
                          So the Court cleared,
And we, no longer held, at once set sail
We ran the colours up with guns and cheered.
With ebb to help us and a topsail gale
By midnight we could see the lights of France,
By cockcrow we were running past the Foreland.